A Faith-Based Approach to

The Divine Time Solution

HOW TO HAVE MORE PEACE, PATIENCE, AND PRODUCTIVITY IN YOUR BUSY MOM LIFE

Danielle Thienel

Table of Contents

Introduction

I want to start off by letting you know two things. One, is that you are not alone with the struggle you experience between life and the clock. And two, I've already been praying for you — the mom that will benefit from what I'm about to share within these pages.

This is for you, mama.

For the mom who has a lot on her plate and whose time is stretched very thin;

For the mom who isn't making the time to care for herself and is juggling a million things (probably with many kids around your ankles or middle schoolers with crazy schedules).

This is even for the mom who has an empty nest but isn't feeling purposeful with the time she does have these days—

I welcome you to Divine Time.

I'm so glad you're here because it tells me that you're ready to take back control of your time, probably after trying all the other usual go-to quick fixes that don't last and have you right back in the same place as before. I created this book for the mom who asked God for help to stop feeling stressed, behind, and overwhelmed with all that there is to do in your life and for your family's lives.

After a profound experience with overwhelm myself and then experiencing great sadness as my best friend was called to heaven too early in her busy mom life (I'll share more about this in Chapter 4), I was forever changed in how I approach time. I took these two experiences along with the expertise I've gained through life coaching busy moms for the past 5 years and I prayed for guidance and wisdom to create and share with you the solution here I call Divine Time.

I continue today to pray to God to ask Him to help me connect this solution with whom He wills as a perfect fit for what is shared here in this book and I hope you will find comfort knowing that you are here as an answer to that prayer. It is my aim that this book, and the concept of Divine Time, will be thought of as an answer to your prayer for time management solutions too.

Inside these pages, you are provided with everything you need to change your relationship with time, to take back control of your time, and to start using your precious time to live a life of less stress and overwhelm. Instead of always being at the mercy of time, you'll be equipped to live a life with more peace and confidence within the areas you choose to spend your time.

You see, I'm a busy mom just like you. I fully understand the challenges that come with it. I'm also a certified life coach, and a member of the Catholic Church which means that my faith plays a very important role in my life and business—it's the cornerstone for all that I do.

My time is filled with my faith practices, activities to support my mental and emotional well being, my husband, my children, my home as well as my work life — a life coaching practice where my mission is focused on helping other faith-filled moms maximize their full potential to have a peaceful, joyful, and balanced motherhood. Divine Time is an essential ingredient to all of us in order to carry out that mission.

In fact, in my first book *The Cyclone Mom Method®: How to Call Upon Your God-Given Power to Remain Calm, In Control, and Confident as a Busy Mom,* the fifth step of this method is to take control of your time. It's so vital to the success of a busy mom-life, I've decided to dedicate a whole book solely on how to do this. *The Divine Time Solution* is that book.

As you read it, if you find at any point you discover that you would like additional support, please don't hesitate to be in touch. I can help you. It all starts with an email to danielle@daniellethienel.com or visit www. daniellethienel.com.

Here is what you'll encounter within the pages of this book:

Part 1 is all about how you view time. You'll experience a shift in how you think about time as you learn about its divine nature. This part provides you with a solid foundation for action, which begins in Part 2.

Part 2 begins with what I call your 'time bombs' — those activities that steal your time and leave you feeling like you don't have enough hours in the day. I even include a full chapter dedicated to technology and how you can wield your time on the screen to create more presence in your life. Part 2 ends with your very own 3-step Divine Time Saver Process.

As we enter Part 3, you'll learn the tools to create your own personalized Divine Time System. In this section, you'll learn how to make time for your faith, yourself, and the responsibilities and dreams within your family, home, and work lives. Part 3 focuses on helping you find balance among the many hats you wear as a mother and woman of faith.

We end the book with my best practices to maintain your Divine Time System and adjust it as life continues forward. You will enjoy peace, patience, and productivity as you live your life through a divine lens.

When you've got a challenge that you're meeting or a circumstance that you didn't expect that you're trying to handle, what tends to happen is we dive in unassisted. We act as if we can handle all of these matters alone.

Yet it would be so much better to approach everything—and I mean everything—in a humble dependence on Christ. Whenever we're feeling tempted to dive into our lives, I urge you to pause and consider a new way to show up in your life that is more Divine.

Stop, turn to Him, and ask Him to show you the way forward.

As we are taking that time, we are connecting and being in his loving presence, which He delights in. He delights in hearing those words that we are asking for his help. And then He answers with, I will guide you along the best pathway for today and for your life.

Before I send you off into what I hope will be a whole new approach for you to successfully reclaim your time back, I would be doing every mom who reads this book a disservice if I didn't also tell you these hard truths. Without taking the steps that I provide in these pages, which I believe is the answer to reclaiming back control of your time, then it's quite possible:

Your plate will always be full.
Your perpetual busyness will never end.
Time will always be something you are battling against.

And maybe the hardest aspect of all is…
You'll miss out on the calm and joyful motherhood God desires for you to experience.

So, to help ensure the changes you want to come to fruition sooner than later, let's not put The Divine Time Solution off any longer and we'll begin in the best way I know how:

In the name of the Father, and of the Son, and of The Holy Spirit, let's get started

Danielle

PART 1

Seeing Time as a Gift

CHAPTER 1

The Concept of Divine Time

You know how sometimes it feels like you have way too much to do and you can't seem to find enough time in the day to do everything on your plate?

This is something we commonly experience as moms, no matter what stage of parenting we're in. Little people need constant care and attention that often interferes with our meals and sleep. Older children need rides and extracurricular support in addition to a new kind of care and attention when compared to their younger years. Teenagers need guided independence in a way that somehow *still* interferes with your meals and sleep. And all the while you're raising these beautiful human beings, you're caring for your spouse, your home, perhaps an outside job, and your own dreams and wellbeing.

It's no wonder we can often feel like we have too much on our plates to manage stress, connect more within our relationships, participate in faith activities, or even just having our own time regularly set aside to rest and recharge.

Divine Time is the solution. It's a plan that helps busy moms, especially those who follow their faith, to manage their time and tasks better. Think of it like having a special guide that shows you how to make the most of your day. It's not just about doing things quickly—it's about doing the *right* things at the right time so you feel happy and less stressed.

Think of it like planning the perfect picnic day. You know exactly what you've brought, when to eat, what games you'll play, and that your purpose is to have relaxation time and fun with those with you. You arrive prepared for the day with the expectations necessary to have a fun and relaxing time.

This is what it's like to abide by Divine Time. This solution helps moms figure out how to balance everything in their lives just like that perfect picnic plan. And if something unexpected happens, like it starts raining or an additional friend shows up, the Divine Time Solution helps you easily adjust your plans smoothly so no matter what, you can handle those curve balls and still enjoy your day.

Divine Time teaches moms how to do this with their everyday lives, helping them feel peaceful and in control even when things are busy or tough.

Here's another way to look at it. You know how we have clocks and schedules that tell us when to wake up, get the kids on the bus for school, start cooking dinner, and so on? We have tools that help us know what time it is and what we need to do when.

But within the concept of Divine Time, we put a focus on time being a special gift from God. Because the truth is, God—who created everything!—also created time. It's a beautiful present He gave us so we can do all the things we love and want to do.

When we think about time as being a gift from God, it will help us use it more wisely and appreciate it more. Divine Time is a special plan that helps busy moms, but especially those who love and follow God, to remember that time is a gift.

When we think about time this way, we feel like there is more time in our day and we don't feel rushed or stressed when going about our tasks. It helps us plan out our day to make sure we have time for everything and that everything fits as perfectly as it can. Even more important, it reminds us to include time for praying, thinking about God, and feeling thankful for all the moments we have here on earth.

If we approach our days this way, it can make our days feel longer and more peaceful—just like God intended for us to experience.

When we see time as a gift from God and use it wisely, we can find more joy in each moment while feeling like we have plenty of time for everything that is important to us.

Divine Time is a special way of thinking about time that comes from understanding how God wants us to live our days instead of just following the clock.

It helps us feel more peaceful and happy with how we use our time. With Divine Time, you're not just thinking about what you need to do next, you're also thinking about what makes you feel happy and close to God.

It's like having a superpower that helps you decide what's really important while ensuring you have time for those things without feeling stressed or hurried.

For example, when you have a busy day with responsibilities piling up with your children, your vocation, your church service, and your own needs, incorporating the concept of Divine Time helps you find moments to relax, pray, and enjoy the little things that make you happy. **It teaches**

you to balance everything in a way that feels just right, not too busy and not too slow.

Instead of just following the clock, Divine Time helps you live your day in a way that feels really good and meaningful. It's like having a secret recipe for a perfect day—every day. Wouldn't that just be amazing?

So how do you practice Divine Time to feel like you have more time without being rushed?

We start by taking an inner look at ourselves, evaluating our outside results, and then begin making really strong and intentional decisions in and around what you see. Making strong decisions is a vital part of the process!

This level of strong decision-making will align with what lights you up, what feels right, and what spiritual and core values you carry within your heart. It will have you being more deliberate and intentional about what you're choosing to think about time, the priorities you set around time, and the ownership of actions you choose to take within the God-given amount of time you have.

I invite you to reevaluate the decisions you make about how you spend your time. And I urge those decisions to be based upon what Scripture teaches us about what is most important, what the commandments tell us to do, and the guidance we receive from God when making these decisions.

If you're in any way like me, you're ready to be given all the steps and eager to dive right into action and get going with handling time better. But before we get started, there is a crucial discussion that needs to happen to ensure we're on the same page. First, we'll walk through a necessary foundation to understand what our most precious resource, which is time, really is.

CHAPTER 2

The Truth About Time

L et's take a moment and step back to the basics.

Here is the truth: time is a mental construct. That's all it is. Time just exists and our experience of it is caused by what we make up in our mind about it. **In other words, time is whatever we think it is.**

Our internal interpretation of time takes place inside of our minds. **Our thoughts ultimately produce the experience we have with time.**

Take a moment to let that sink in. I'm guessing this is quite different from how you generally think about time as a construct in your day. For most people, the belief is that time is something that we're at the effect of, that it isn't expandable, and that we are ruled by it...

But that's not the case.

The truth is that we each choose to think and create our experience of time. If we believe time is our friend, granting us the space and freedom to pursue our passions or create memories with those we love, that's what we will experience. But that's not usually how we feel about time.

We often see time as a necessary evil, forever marching forward slow and relentless in its cadence, robbing us of our good health, our golden days, and our ability to check-off the items on our neverending to-do list.

If we believe time is against us, an easy scapegoat to blame when things don't go our way, we walk around seeing time as scarce, lacking abundance.

The scarcity and abundance of the time we each have doesn't and can't come from the external parameters that society has set around it. We often think of time as something that is outside of our control, but the truth is *each of us is the source of time.* **We are the ones who decide how to use our time and how to make the most of it.**

In other words, our experience of time is up to us. What we choose to think about it is what will make us feel better about the time we have at any moment. This is fantastic news because we no longer have to put blame on the clock! **The control of expansion or limitations within time are our own to do with as we please.**

As we discuss these truths about time, it is important to remember that time is our most precious resource. Some of us believe that time is second to money in a hierarchy of our resources, but that is not the case. Unlike money, if we run out of time, we can't make more of it, whereas we can always make more money if we decide to. As a faith-filled human, we see that it is our responsibility to make the most of the time we do have on Earth to care for this gift of life that God gave us and Jesus sacrificed for us.

Time is your most precious resource to care for, **and you show your stewardship in how you spend your time.**

We have less and less time with each passing day, perfectly visualized with an hourglass. When we were born, the sand began to fall. There's nothing we could do to make it stop falling or to push that sand back up into the top of the hourglass.

I don't bring this up for you to be sad about how time is fleeting and we don't know when our last days on earth are. I bring up the truth about time being our most precious resource so that you will feel even more committed to enjoying your life right now and make the most out of the time that you have with this gift of life.

I'm inviting you to place more focus on what matters most to you in how you spend your time that you've been given—for however long that ends up being.

Time is a concept that has been around since the beginning of human civilization. It is a measure of the passing of days, months, and years.

However, as I mentioned before, it's a measurement of the mind. It's a mental construct. The people of our past collectively got together and decided how we would all agree upon how to measure the passage of time.

One of the earliest ways of measuring time was by observing the movement of the stars and the seasons in ancient civilizations. The calendar was based on the movements of the moon and the sun with days and months being marked by the phases of the moon and the changing seasons.

The 24-hour day is a concept first used by the Babylonians who divided the day into 24 equal parts. This was then adopted by the Romans who used it to measure the passing of time. The 24-hour day has since become the standard way of measuring time in most parts of the world.

Beyond the 24-hour cycle, our ancestors used the seasons to measure the passage of time. This gave way to the invention of the Sundial in the 13th century, then the mechanical clock became the best method to keep time.

These clocks then became miniaturized and portable as wearable watches, which progressed into the technologies of today where our smartphones keep us constantly attached to each hour and minute of the day.

And although the truth is that these collective ways to measure time were built with the intentions of helping us, they also overshadowed our own abilities to use our God-given agency within our own minds to create what we truly want—which includes how we feel about and use time.

In his book *The Big Leap,* Gay Hendrix discusses the concept of time and how it affects our lives. He argues that time is a relative experience and that our relationship with time can have a significant impact on our productivity, happiness, and overall well being. One of the key points that Hendrix makes about time is that we often approach it in a scarcity mindset. We feel like we don't have enough time to do everything we want to do, and as a result, we often rush through our activities and become stressed and overwhelmed.

Hendricks suggests that we need to shift our mindset from scarcity to abundance. When it comes to time, we need to recognize that time is a limitless resource and we can always create more of it by changing our relationship with it. By approaching time with a sense of abundance, we can reduce stress and increase our productivity.

Another point that Hendricks makes is that we often use time as an excuse for not pursuing our goals or dreams. We say things like, "I don't have enough time," or, "I'll do it when I have more time."

The reality is that we often have more time than we think. Hendricks suggests that we need to take responsibility for how we use our time and prioritize the things that matter most to us. This is exactly what I teach as part of The Divine Time Solution found in this book.

Finally, Hendricks argues that time is a subjective experience. We can stretch time or compress it depending on our mental state and level of engagement with what we're doing. He calls this concept "Einstein Time" after Albert Einstein, who believed that time was a relative construct and not an absolute constant. By fully engaging with what we're doing and being fully present in the moment, we can expand our experience of time and accomplish much more in less time.

Our relationship with time is critical to our success and happiness, and this book sets out to help you strengthen your relationship with time. **We can make the most of this precious resource by shifting our mindset and taking responsibility for our relationship with time.** This change in the approach will create a more fulfilling life.

If you were to adopt what I offer in this chapter, just this one bit of knowledge can change everything for you. I can remember myself being exposed to this new way of looking at time and having it just blow my mind wide open in a way that provided so much comfort and possibility.

This intellectual understanding of time is a huge step in the right direction, but it still falls short because it lacks the divine perspective of our most precious resource—which is exactly where we're headed next.

CHAPTER 3

The Divine Time Difference

As Christians, we have a different view of what it means to use our time wisely because of how our faith, which is the foundation for all we do, impacts our life's focus. Our ultimate goal is to get to Eternity through our love for Christ. The desire to follow His teachings and His example are what are at the forefront of our mind when we are living by Divine Time and inform how we choose to spend our time.

The Catholic Church, the faith I belong to, acknowledges time as a fundamental aspect of human experience, even developing various teachings and practices related to time. You would likely agree that one who is Christian and follows their church teachings and activities would have a different focus of where to spend their time than someone who isn't affiliated with a church or its customs.

For example, in my faith, one of the most significant teachings of the Catholic Church about time is its emphasis on the Liturgical Year. This way of measuring time provides me a framework for worship and spirituality, and it helps Catholics to remember and participate in the major events of Salvation History.

In addition to the Liturgical Year, the Catholic church also teaches the importance of time in individual spiritual practices such as prayer and reflection. We are encouraged to set aside regular times for prayer and reflection, in addition to weekly mass and other sacramental practices.

As busy moms who want to be an example for our children and engage them in our faith, we know that our time includes going to mass, participating in the sacraments, making time to pray the rosary, as well as allotting time for our children's faith education, particularly during sacramental year activities like a First Holy Communion or Confirmation year.

The church also teaches the importance of using time wisely to fulfill one's purpose and serve God. We are called to be good stewards of time and to use it in ways that honor God like being of service to others.

Divine Time is the approach that encourages us to make the most of our opportunities to do this. As Christians, we believe that God is the creator of everything, including time. In Genesis 1: 1-5, we read, "God created the heavens and the earth and separated the light from the darkness."

This act of separating light from darkness can be seen as God creating the first concept of time. Therefore, time is a gift from God, and because we desire to be good stewards of this gift, we are called to use it wisely and responsibly.

If you are feeling out of sorts in your time management, it may be simply because you have forgotten how divine the time we have on earth is; that time is truly a precious gift.

When we view time as a gift, we become more intentional about how we use it. We can prioritize our activities and focus on the things that matter most to us, such as spending time with our families, serving others, and pursuing our passions.

However, managing time can be challenging. It's easy to get caught up in the busyness of life and forget to focus on what's truly important when there are sports activities to drive the kids to, food to prepare, laundry to put away, and many more tasks and responsibilities that vie for our time.

It's hard to keep our minds from believing that it's all so important, but in fact, only a few things truly matter to spend your time on. That's why it's essential to approach time management with a Christian perspective.

We can see so many examples of these truths in scripture verses and stories.

One of my favorite scriptures that teaches part of the concept of Divine Time can be found in Ecclesiastes 3: 1–8, "For everything, there is a season and a time for every matter under heaven, a time to plant, time to pluck what is planted."

This passage teaches us that there is a proper time for everything. It encourages us to recognize and honor the different seasons of our lives, which beautifully resonate with the idea that we experience different seasons of motherhood. Through this scripture, we understand that each stage, each moment, has its purpose. There will be challenging times, but there will also be incredible, breathtaking times. I hope that learning about Divine Time will help you focus on what is fun and good about each season of your life.

Another one of my favorite scriptures around this topic is found in Psalms 90:12, "Number our days that we would get a heart of wisdom."

This scripture teaches us to focus on the fact that we have a certain number of days on the earth. It helps us value our time so we will use it wisely, and it encourages us to make thoughtful and meaningful choices with the time that we do have.

This brings us to Galatians 6:9, "And let us not grow weary of doing good for in due season, We will reap if we do not give up."

For me, I experience this in the sense of coaching. I love this scripture and its reminder to persevere and not grow weary. It takes patience to live life like that. It teaches us to trust in God's timing and to continue on our way, knowing that we will see the fruits of our labor in due time.

Another scriptural example of Divine Time can be found in Matthew 6: 33–34, "But seek first the kingdom of God in His righteousness and all these things will be added to you. Therefore, do not be anxious about tomorrow, for tomorrow will be anxious for itself. Sufficient for the day is its own trouble."

Of course, this teaches us to prioritize our spiritual life and to trust God with our future. It focuses on aligning our daily actions with our faith, admonishing us to let go of unnecessary worries about the future.

Divine Time takes into account that our lives need to have a different perspective than others who don't have Christ at the center of their lives.

We can turn to the Bible for guidance on how to use our time effectively. In Ephesians 5: 15–16, the Apostle Paul urges us to be wise in how we use our time making the most of every opportunity. We can also look to Jesus who frequently took time to pray and spend time alone with his disciples, even in the midst of his busy ministry. When I study scripture, I see how much He made it a priority to rest and recharge so he could handle His continuous ministry.

We can also look to the Bible story of Jesus and Lazareth to learn about Divine TIme.

In this scriptural story, Jesus heard that Lazareth was ill, but He waited to visit. It was a total of four days (to our human reckoning of time) and, of course, everyone treated Lazareth as if he were dead. The capacity of the human mind could not comprehend any other outcome. Friends of Jesus looked at his late arrival as bad timing. They thought it was a shame that Lazareth died so close to Jesus's arrival and that he shouldn't have been allowed to die. They even commented on how his body is decomposing and starting to stink.

But Jesus, understanding more than we do, called Lazareth forth from the dead. Lazareth arose out of what was intended to be his final resting place and lived, serving God all his days.

This story illustrates that our expectations may not line up with God's timing. There was a greater purpose to the delay of Jesus that no one other than Jesus could see at the time! It teaches us to have faith and trust that God's timing is always for the best, even when it might involve waiting or having delays in our lives. Divine Time is not the earthly expectation of instant gratification. Blessings and good things will come according to God's timetable.

When talking about Divine Time, we can even consider the story about the birth of Jesus. He was sent down to earth at the exact time God intended Him to be here. The same is true for you!

Divine Time continues to circle back to the main concept that time is of God. We can see how he orchestrated the events for the birth of Jesus and how that timing aligned with His greater plan.

These passages remind us that to live by Divine Time is to trust God's timing. As we mentioned earlier, it all starts with how you look at it—namely recognizing God's timing. Just as He planned the timing of Jesus' birth, He orchestrates the significant events in our own lives.

There are many more scriptural examples in living life by Divine Time as opposed to the limited view we learn in the course of our human existence. Now the question is how can we apply these biblical principles to our time management? What are the exact steps to take so we can feel this sacred, peaceful way about our time?

The total of what's offered in this book will help you do just that. What I want to be your big takeaway from this lesson is that **time is a precious gift from God, and we should manage it with intention and purpose by using a Christian perspective.**

Our time is divine. It's of God and from God. Let that be the main driver of what you do and don't do with your time. We can make the most of our time and live a fulfilling and purposeful life that aligns with all of our goals throughout each busy stage of motherhood.

This may seem like a stretch for some of you. I know I felt this way a number of years ago. The concept of God's timing made for a nice homily, but could it really affect my daily life in any profound way?

The answer, my friend—for you and me—is yes.

CHAPTER 4

The Reality of Divine Time

A number of years ago, I was not using the Divine Time steps and principles as they are taught in this book. I was focused on earthly productivity, success, and validation in my motherhood. I said yes to everything because of the people-pleasing and the perfectionist qualities I used to carry around.

I was always striving for perfection while saying yes to things that weren't priorities. I took on too much and filled my time with everything that I thought I was supposed to do or what would make me happy—which meant I was not a firm decision maker. And I certainly was not asking God for His assistance and clarity while lighting my path forward.

In short, I was doing everything I thought a good mom was *supposed* to do—no matter the consequence. Does that sound familiar to you?

I packed my time full of tasks without stopping to evaluate my priorities. I strove to be a good wife, mom, daughter, and worker without considering any aspect of Divine Time.

During this time I worked outside of my home. I had three kids living under my roof, which meant there were a lot of school and sports activities.

I took on a home renovation and moved my parents across the street so I could take care of them…while simultaneously keeping up with my own household. I also did what I could to maintain my relationships with friends and those outside of my immediate circle.

Of course, my spiritual life was present. I went to church and participated in activities, but the priorities weren't aligned. I wasn't calling on God. I wasn't thinking about life choices from a heavenly perspective. I wasn't evaluating what truly mattered when piling tasks onto my to-do list. As many of us do, I had misconceptions about needing outside resources to better manage my time and productivity.

I thought things like, "You're going to Target to get the next best awesome planner so you can *finally* juggle all the things and do them really well." Sound familiar?

Well, I got sick. And not just let-me-down-some-medicine-and-keep-on-with-my-day sick, I got knocked down flat for two whole weeks.

Two weeks of no work, no shuttling the kids around to their activities, no favors to friends or family. I had two weeks of sitting, thinking, pondering, and—for the first time in a long time— time to consider what was truly important in my life.

I was forced to slow down. I was forced to reevaluate and reprioritize my life. I definitely had time to consider my own thoughts and see what was going on inside my head. I realized that I wasn't feeling great about some things in my life and the choices I had made about my time. I had some decisions —and changes—to make.

But before I did that, I listened.

I remember the day I went back to work. I sat back down at my computer and as I started to boot it up, I heard the Holy Spirit. The Holy Spirit spoke to me. I had quieted myself enough when I was sick to recognize that I heard the spirit's voice and the message was that I was more needed at home than I was at my job. I already knew in my heart that it was the right thing for me and listening to The Holy Spirit would align my priorities with my current stage of motherhood.

That began the switch to operating by Divine Time as opposed to earthly time. As I made decisions about the busyness I had in life, I called on the Spirit and asked for help. Once I was home, I began to add things to my time that were important and mattered.

These were things like dedicating more time to prayer, reading the Bible, exercise, catching up with friends, and participating more fully in church activities and sacraments. These were things that lit me up, filled my cup, and made me feel better. As I began to feel better, I then had the energy and joy to show up more in service for my family and lovingly help with their needs and desires.

My time and my relationship with time was more divinely led. As I continued, I found that my organization and time management were more effective. I not only felt like I had more time each day, but that I was using that time for good.

As I have continued to use these concepts of Divine Time, I have found myself in the position to say yes to the right opportunities that allow me to grow closer to God and enjoy my own personal growth—the things that are delightful to me. I have been present with my children, who are now grown. I spent years with my parents before my father joined God in heaven.

I am forever grateful for the experience of getting as sick as I did because it forced me to stop living life at the mercy of the chaos around me and instead put me back in the driver's seat so I could evaluate and choose a more divine way of living.

Even while I was nurturing my spiritual self, I learned yet another valuable lesson about Divine TIme when my best friend passed away at a young age.

Jill was my closest friend. In fact, she is in my baby book as my first friend ever! When we were younger, we spent time together every summer playing and dreaming and all the things young children do. Time seemed so abundant because we had so much joy when we were together.

Jill and I were always close. We both got married and started our families. Fast forward to the time when both of us were in our forties. We both had three young children. And she got diagnosed with breast cancer.

This turned into a three year battle that she eventually lost. At the time of this writing, Jill has been absent from the earth for five years. And yet, I still think about the insights and interactions I received from her during that time.

She knew her time was limited, but there was always a spark of hope alive in the way she spoke to me. Even at the end, when it was clear that she would not beat her battle with cancer, she had such wonderful things to share with me. She would make references that underscored the urgency to make the most of this life and the time we have.

For example, Jill and I grew up swimming together in my family's pool. When my husband and I got married and moved into the home we currently live in, we always said that our yard was perfect for a pool. And then life happened. Kids needed school supplies and activities, work got busy, and before we knew it, the pool got pushed to the backburner.

But as my best friend, she knew that I had always wanted a pool for my family. She listened as I would say, "One day when we have a pool…" too many times to count. So when she was in the hospital, knowing the end was near, the first thing she asked was, "*NOW* are you going to get your pool?"

She knew that waiting for tomorrow would end up meaning I would wait too long. This was a desire of my heart and she taught me not to put it off.

As I reflect on this story, I am sitting next to the pool in my backyard. It's summertime and there's a lovely breeze.

Jill didn't necessarily mean that I needed a pool. Period. Done.

She wanted to remind me that I might not always be here, that we are never promised tomorrow. That life is short, so some things shouldn't wait.

After she asked me that question and heard me offer an excuse yet again, she cocked her head to the side, opened her eyes really wide and said, "Danielle, get the darn pool already."

So I did. I went to God and prayed over the decision. If it was still in my heart to have a pool, could He help make that happen? Could I trust that the funds would fall into place one way or another? Could He help me see the joy in this project?

We went ahead with it and God provided. We have had years of wonderful family times in our pool and have made beautiful memories with many more to come.

I don't know that I would have pushed myself to do that if not for Jill. She knocked me straight into a powerful lesson about Divine Time. It's less about the limited time we have on this earth, and more about living now in the abundant, heavenly way God intended us to experience time.

I thank God daily for my family, for friends like Jill, and for the experiences that remove our earthly blinders—even for a moment—so we can live more divinely aligned with God and His time.

PART 2

How to Manage Time Challenges

CHAPTER 5

Diffuse Your Time Bombs

I understand the unique challenges you face in balancing your faith, family, and personal aspirations. In this chapter, we'll explore a crucial concept that often stands between you and the effective use of your time. We call it the time bomb.

Because let's face it, it's a fitting name for exactly what happens to us. We set out with our perfectly laid out schedule and then—BOOM!—something comes up and explodes that plan.

I first learned the term 'time bomb' from Dave Durand. It's defined as something that lurks within your schedule, ready to explode and sabotage your best laid plans. It's a sneaky culprit that keeps you from using your time as you truly desire.

These time bombs can manifest in various forms and they differ for each of us. They can be external factors, internal struggles, or even unexpected events that threaten to derail our daily routines and steal precious moments from our lives.

You may have recognized some time bombs for yourself, but there are others you may encounter without even realizing it. You can fall prey to them without being conscious of it—but that is what we can change right now, in the next few chapters.

Picture those instances when you desperately want to have a few moments of quiet time, but a never ending to-do list demands your attention, or when you have grand plans for quality time with your family only to be bombarded by unexpected phone calls or mental distractions from unfinished tasks.

These time bombs have the power to disrupt our mental, emotional, and spiritual lives as well as our relationships and our patience, peace, and productivity.

In other words, time bombs can disrupt our overall personal well being!

But fear not my dear friends, because I will arm you with the tools and strategies to overcome these challenges and reclaim your time. Below, you'll find the 10 most common time bombs for moms and how to tackle those time bombs head on.

These time bombs are the barriers standing between you and the life you envision for yourself; a life filled with purpose, faith, and using your time as you want. When you understand what your personal time bombs are and how to disarm them, you can create a roadmap for Divine Time management to help yourself reclaim the control and peace you deserve.

The Top 10 Time Bombs Busy Moms Face

Before we dive in, let's be real here. While I am speaking to moms of faith, these are actually all the same things that get in the way of any mom's desire to use her time wisely. We want to always have our faith values and principles top of mind—from the things we do to what we're involved in.

Our time is a gift from God and as such, we want to be good stewards of it.

Each of these time bombs presents a unique challenge, but fear not because armed with the awareness of what they are and the mindfulness to strategize around them, you'll be equipped to begin to overcome each time bomb that plagues your day.

Procrastination

Procrastination, the tempting allure of delaying our tasks and putting off important responsibilities until later... We've all been there, haven't we? When you have a list of errands to run, bills to pay, and chores to complete, but instead you find yourself scrolling through social media or engrossed in a TV show—that's procrastination. It steals our precious time and often leaves us scrambling at the last minute or doing some other "easier" activity that has us avoiding the hard thing our brain doesn't want to do.

Indecision

Indecision can be paralyzing, causing a challenge when making choices or taking decisive action. It's like being caught between two paths, unable to move forward with either one.

I remember a coaching client who struggled with indecision when it came to selecting the best extracurricular activities for her children. After all, she thought, there are so many to choose from! She placed such pressure on herself when she would think it had to be done right and be the perfect choice. She had to pick the right one because it might affect what they're going to be when they grow up!

She spent hours talking about it, thinking about it, seeking advice, and questioning her choices—which only added to her stress while wasting valuable time.

Indecision kept her stuck from even trying one out. She didn't consider picking one to see if it turned out to be the right one. Pivoting later if an extracurricular didn't work out wasn't on her radar.

Indecision keeps you stuck from moving forward. Making any choice, even if it yields an answer you don't want, is still better and time-enhancing over the indecision that takes you nowhere.

Distractions and Interruptions

We live in an age of constant distractions. From phone notifications to household chores or unexpected visits from friends, these distractions can derail our focus and rob us of precious time.

Picture this scenario. You sit down to tackle an important project or engage in prayer, but your phone buzzes with notifications, demanding your attention, or perhaps your children need your immediate assistance while you're trying to concentrate. These distractions and interruptions can prevent you from effectively using your time.

Stress and Overwhelm

As moms, we often carry the weight of multiple responsibilities like juggling our family's needs, work obligations, and personal aspirations. This can lead to stress and overwhelm, making it difficult to manage our time effectively. I personally struggle with stress and overwhelm as a busy Catholic mom; my to-do list seems never ending. I can often feel pulled in multiple directions and stress and overwhelm were certainly what was sabotaging my time and productivity goals.

I remember a time when it felt like I couldn't catch a break, let alone manage my time efficiently. I blamed everything outside of me: my boss, the contractor fixing the house, and my kids' packed schedules to name a few.

I let stress and overwhelm rule me instead of being mindful about who the creator of time is, where time came from, and ultimately that I'm the one responsible to create the time that I need and want.

Relaxed Deadlines

When we don't set clear deadlines or allow flexibility without accountability, tasks can stretch out indefinitely, creating a false sense that we have plenty of time for ourselves.

Have you ever experienced this? You tell yourself, "Oh, I'll get to it eventually." Only to find days turn into weeks, weeks turn into months with tasks left unfinished. Relaxed deadlines can undermine our productivity and leave us feeling unaccomplished.

Having a goal or deadline of time to accomplish something actually gives your brain a perimeter to shoot for—a direction, a focus. This can increase your time efficiency and ultimately undermine the time bomb of relaxed deadlines.

Perfectionism

As moms, we strive to give our best in all aspects of our lives. While it may seem admirable, perfectionism can become a time consuming trap.

This is definitely something I struggled with before coaching, and I didn't see at the time how perfectionism was filling my time with an "always striving yet never arriving" way. It zapped my time goal efforts.

I had a client who struggled with perfectionism as well. She often found herself spending excessive amounts of time perfecting every detail of a project, whether it was preparing a meal or organizing an event. She felt an immense pressure to meet impossibly high standards. This perfectionism not only consumed her time, but also left her exhausted and unfulfilled.

Perfectionists will constantly sabotage their time. The reason is because the pursuit of perfection uses an exorbitant amount of time while going after a means that never comes to an end. "Perfect" for us humans only comes after this human life and in eternity.

People Pleasing

As moms, we have big hearts and a desire to help and support others. We help constantly and often say, "yes" to every request, yet that can lead us to overwhelming commitments and compromised personal time.

When you are prone to people-pleasing behaviors, you find yourself stretched thin, juggling multiple commitments and obligations because you don't want to disappoint anyone.

People pleasing can drain your energy and prevent you from dedicating time to what truly matters. When you are saying yes to things that you really mean, "no," it's a lie. We lie to ourselves and essentially to others.

Fatigue

As is mentioned in other time bombs, busy moms often put others' needs before their own, neglecting, self-care, and adequate rest. This can lead to physical exhaustion on top of the already mental and emotional exhaustion we might be carrying around. This hinders our ability to use our time effectively. There's simply not the clarity or inspiration needed to show up as our best time manager when we are exhausted.

I remember when a member of my group program pushed herself relentlessly. She would sacrifice sleep and neglected her own wellbeing in pursuit of meeting everyone else's needs, especially her boss with the marketing job that she held.

Only after coaching together did she soon realize that her fatigue was not only affecting her health, but taking her in the exact opposite direction of her life's mission and the focus she wanted to dedicate elsewhere during this season of motherhood.

Electronics

In today's digital age, electronic devices can be both a blessing and a curse when it comes to our time management. This is one of the major time bombs that I coach on in my practice. I want to bring it into your awareness, too.

I imagine that even if you only focused on this one time bomb, it could be a big help to your time management. We've all experienced it, right? A quick glance at our phones for a moment of distraction that ends up turning into hours spent mindlessly scrolling through social media or getting lost in online content.

Electronics can steal our time and distract us from our priorities. It's definitely something you want to be aware of and make some goals around so we can tackle it head on.

Time Versus Money

One way we often overlook to gain control of our time is to use money in exchange for time. When there are time bombs sabotaging you or when you feel there isn't enough time or that you aren't using your time wisely, there is an option to pay for someone else to complete a task or take an activity off your plate to save you time.

In our society, we are taught the value of money. We see a ten dollar bill and place value on it. We know what $100 or $1000 can get us and we're constantly evaluating worth in terms of the almighty dollar. But with that as our focus, we miss the value of time. We don't see time through a divine lens, as a resource with its own value.

In fact, time is more valuable than money because money is a renewable resource, time is not. If you lose all your money, you can build it up again. There is not a finite amount of money in your life. Whereas time is exactly the opposite. It's impossible to get back the time that you've spent because time is finite. Time is a much more valuable resource because it is not renewable.

Understanding this truth about time and money, one way to diffuse a time bomb is to look at your schedule and determine what you might want to exchange time for money. What to-do list items are worth outsourcing for a few dollars to free up your time?

The classic example I like to use to demonstrate this principle is cleaning my house, which would cost me five hours of my time twice a month. That comes to ten hours per month I could have for something else I needed time for. Even if I only clean my home once a month in this way, that five hours could be precious time spent elsewhere.

If I decided I wanted to free up those ten hours each month to spend more time with my young children, pursue a second career, or simply have less stress in my life, I could make that choice by paying someone to clean my house during that time. I can choose to exchange currency for time while still having a clean house. Considering exchanging money for time is a useful strategy if you want to add more time back into your schedule.

When we consider Divine Time, we see that time is a gift and we can't get back lost or used time. I encourage you to be aware of that truth when you make choices about how you use a renewable resource, like money, to free up more of a nonrenewable resource, like time.

After you complete a time audit, it can be a helpful exercise to go through and simply identify the areas that you could potentially exchange paying someone else to take that task off your plate. If you choose to outsource any of your tasks to gain more time, then prioritize that time on something else more aligned with your mission statement, which we will craft in the coming pages.

—

Each of these time bombs presents its own set of challenges. In a couple of chapters, we'll explore what your personal time bombs are and talk through the strategy necessary to overcome them.

However, before we dive into fixing everything, we first need to understand a powerful tool that helps us break down and understand what is actually happening inside our own minds, that is the reason for whether we are using your time divinely or not. This tool is called The Model.

CHAPTER 6

The Model to Manage Your Time

The Model is the number one tool I use to help my clients gain awareness of the things that are holding them back.

This tool is a framework that brings you clarity to what you are actively creating for yourself in all the different situations of your life. It is particularly useful to help you move closer to creating a life lived by Divine Time.

Once you have clarity over your roadblocks, this tool will empower you to get clarity over obstacles, identify needed adjustments, and ultimately move closer to what you want. It focuses on your mindset and the principles that underlie whether we feel like we have enough time to do the things we want, or if we are not getting what we want out of our schedules and our time.

The official name of the tool that I'm using is the Self-Coaching Model, and I refer to it as The Model for short. It's powerful and effective in helping you be more peaceful, patient, and productive. In regard to Divine Time management, it's vital to get inside your own mind and understand the mental and emotional experiences that are being created in there.

I have found that this tool, The Model, works better than anything else I have come across. I learned this from Brooke Castillo and the Life Coach School, where I am certified from. This is the foundational tool we use as mindset coaches and it gets tremendous results for our clients.

I've dug deep into this tool and learned many of the nuances within the Model, and I'm still learning how to apply it in new and different ways. All of this to say—I'm going to teach you the basics of The Model and show you how it can greatly help you manage your time.

Your life is a bit of a math equation, and I love that because math equations can be solved! The Model turns situations into a simplified equation. It allows you to coach yourself through whatever you're experiencing.

It's a simple tool, and the simplicity is my favorite part of it. It's not complicated, it's not fancy. It beautifully breaks down any situation, including "time situations" into five basic categories. It goes like this:

Circumstance

This is your situation in life or what is currently happening. Circumstances are always facts, whether those have to do with your life or with what's going on around you at the moment. Since they are facts, they can be proven. These are things like how many kids you have, the things on your to-do list to be completed, how many hours left in the day, etc. These are facts that can be proved, like having a husband can be proved as a fact with a marriage certificate. Having a ten-year-old is an example of a fact because it can be proved with a birth certificate.

Circumstances are the things that all the world would agree to as being true and factual. Circumstances would also include the words and actions of people. When you "see" or define the circumstances of your life it would be very boring and neutral, lacking any descriptive words.

If I said I was a Catholic mom who is writing a book, everyone would agree on it. Those are facts. When using The Model, it's most helpful to define your circumstance as specific, boring, plain, and neutral as possible.

If you're struggling to sleep at night, the circumstance part of The Model could say something like, "There are 24 hours in a day and I get an average of 4 hours of sleep a night." It is specific, factual, and does not lean on opinion or emotion.

Thought

This is the part of The Model where we bring awareness to our assumptions and interpretations of the facts (what we just listed as a circumstance).

This is where we assign meaning to all those circumstances that we come across in our life. **Thoughts are just sentences and phrases that come in and pass through our minds, many times unconsciously.** And though you might not have looked at it in this way before, thoughts are optional.

Thoughts are choices we make. We choose what to think about. We are the ones who decide what thoughts to think and focus on.

For example, let's say we experience a circumstance that there are two hours before preschool ends. You might choose a thought that goes something like this, "That's plenty of time to get the laundry washed, folded and put away." Or you also have the option to choose the thought, "Two hours? That's not enough time to finish. I might as well not even start." Different brains will interpret facts differently.

The circumstance was two hours left before preschool pickup, that's a fact. But the thought that follows is optional.

Our thoughts are the most important key to efficient and effective time management.

Recall the truth that time is a mental construct and our experience of time is due to how we choose to think about how we are spending those precious hours of ours.

Well, this principle behind our thinking and the role our thoughts play in our daily experiences is what I'm laser-pointing out to you. Time is a circumstance and you want to give a lot more attention to detail on what you are choosing to think about everything in your life in regards to your time because that is the difference maker to whether it's managed efficiently or not.

Our thoughts are the big differentiator between those who are successful with their time management and those that are not. Our thoughts and thinking patterns are malleable and can be changed. We have control over this, which is such great news!

When you think things like, "I have so much to do. There's never enough time. I'm spread too thin. I'm behind on everything. If only I had more hours in the day..." Those are just thoughts, not facts.

And that difference is the key to everything.

Feeling/ Emotion

So far, we understand that our circumstance is what triggers our thoughts. Circumstances are facts, but thoughts, or the meaning we assign to those circumstances, are optional. It then follows that our thoughts create the emotions we experience.

This part of The Model is most effective when we can distill it down to one word, one emotion. It's the ones you're familiar with like happy, sad, disappointed, excited, motivated, inspired—all of those feelings are actually created from a thought inside of your brain and not by the circumstance itself.

Oftentimes we think that our feelings are a result of what's happening outside of us, and that's probably what you've been thinking up to this point in your life. We tend to jump from a circumstance to our feelings, but that's not actually what is happening. There's a different way to look at what is happening within ourselves and that process is the key to managing our time effectively.

In our earlier example, we listed a circumstance that there are 24 hours in the day and you are sleeping for an average of 4 hours a night. Many people jump straight to the emotion of feeling hopeless, frustrated, or overwhelmed. What they miss is zeroing in on the thoughts they are having about the circumstance (4 hours of sleep in a 24 hour period) and looking at the relationship between those thoughts and the feelings they experience.

Changing your thinking will naturally influence the emotions that follow.

What you've been *thinking* is what has been creating those feelings of frustration, stress, and overwhelm.

So far within The Model, we know that a one word emotion is a result from a thought, which is a sentence or phrase you think in your mind in response to a circumstance, or a fact about your life as it stands right now.

Action

Our feelings are what fuel our actions. Just like a car, having the right gas (or even having gas in the first place) gets us to move forward. Emotions are our fuel and, like a car that won't move well without the right grade of fuel, we won't move without the right emotions driving us.

Even standing still is considered an action. Before learning about mindset work, I used to wish I didn't have to feel my feelings. I wish I wasn't driven by feelings for what I did, but it turns out that is literally not possible.

Our feelings are what fuel us to take action—and that is true for all the actions we take. If you think about your neverending to-do list and feel overwhelmed by all you have to do with your limited time, notice how it then drives you to distract yourself or other behavior that doesn't really move you forward. Compare that to thoughts about your ability to get tasks done and feeling excited, energized, motivated, or inspired. If you felt those things, then your action(s) would look different from the first example. You'd get a lot done!

Please know that how you feel matters a lot because feelings drive actions. How we feel determines what we do and what we don't do. This is important to understand as we go through and create your time plans in Part 3 of this book and set out on following through on those plans.

You have circumstances in your life that trigger a thought, or a series of thoughts, which then creates our feelings, and those feelings drive our actions.

Result

Now the last component of the framework, that began with a circumstance, is the results we create for ourselves. Our actions create results. I'm guessing that you have a good grasp on results and what they look like in your life.

We do things and then that's how we get our results. You already know that when you take the action of working out, you increase your muscles and improve your cardiovascular system. There is an effect to the action of going to the gym to work out. If you choose not to go to the gym, that is also an action with a different result on your health.

This is the part of The Model that most people focus on. Change your action to change the results you experience, period done.

However, I want to help you manage your time in a way that will truly produce results. And that's not found by starting with a focus on the action line. I want you to wrap your brain around the idea, the thing that you haven't necessarily been taught before, that *changing the results you have in life starts with your thoughts.*

Our lives as they stand are a direct reflection of our thoughts. Focusing on the thoughts you choose is going to determine if you ultimately have the results you want in regards to your time. This is where Divine Time begins.

We have this saying inside of my coaching community that you're always going to find evidence for the thoughts you're thinking within your brain. You're always going to see evidence in the results that you have in your life. In other words, what you think and believe is actually what is creating the results you have in your life.

When you're thinking about your to-do list and how productive or restful you want to be, it becomes easier to accomplish that mountain you're climbing. This model makes math out of the way humans operate in the world. It gives us the ability to structure our thoughts, emotions, and actions in a way that leads to the results we want to experience.

I encourage you to start thinking about using The Model on yourself. Maybe organize your time challenges and situations into each of the five categories and attempt to do one model a day, a couple models a week. Any awareness you gain from seeing your life circumstances through the lens of The Model is going to prove fruitful.

And of course, because I offer support beyond this book, if you are interested in working with me personally and see what this model can do with you in any aspect of your life, not just with your time, you can go to www.daniellethienel.com and view my offerings. It is my greatest joy to dive deeper into all being taught here and help my clients (and now you!) experience more peace, patience, and productivity in your busy mom life.

Remember, your circumstances are factual pieces about your life and the situations and experiences you have on a daily basis. We can prove circumstances to be true beyond a shadow of doubt.

Think about the weather in 24 hours. We don't have control over the weather! But we do have control over what we think about the weather when you wake up tomorrow morning—whether it's rainy or straight sunshine. Our thoughts will influence what we feel. Thoughts like, "I hate how hot it is outside!" are sure to rub off on the actions you take on your commute to your daughter's noon gymnastics practice.

Would it be a shock if you were late to gymnastics because you started with that thought? No! But if you get up and choose a different thought, "I am grateful I have air conditioning and a way to listen to my favorite audiobook!" That's sure to create different feelings, actions, and a result you can be proud of.

I hope you use this model in more ways than just applying it to the context of living by Divine Time. Our next chapter will bring back the concept of time bombs by helping you identify the top time bombs you specifically deal with and implementing The Model to create a plan to overcome these time bombs once and for all.

CHAPTER 7

Identify and Overcome Your Time Bombs

Now that you have a greater awareness of what specific obstacles are the most common time bombs, we'll work through how to identify your top time bombs and how you can move forward and overcome them.

As you work through this chapter, I want you to identify your top three time bombs. I know there's a decent chance you could identify more than three, it may be that each one is present in your life! But, for the sake of making great progress, it's better for our brains to be laser-focused on a few things at a time than send it trying to help us overcome every obstacle at once.

You can always work on the other time bombs later, but I urge you to hone in on the top three you think are the most sabotaging for you.

Self-Reflection

The first step in this process is self-reflection. Take a moment to pause and honestly assess your current time management challenges. Grab a notebook and start by making a list of areas in your life where you feel your time is slipping away; where you struggle to find balance or efficiency.

These could be moments when you experience frustration, overwhelm, or a sense of not living up to your own expectations. Are you finding it most difficult to spend your time on your faith, on yourself, on your family, on your home, or on your job?

Once you've identified those areas, it's time to match them with the specific time bombs we've discussed throughout this book. Go through the list of time bombs and see which ones resonate with your personal experiences.

For example, if you find yourself constantly putting off tasks until the last minute and thinking things like, "I'll just do it later," or, "I'm better at waiting until the last minute," then procrastination may be a significant time bomb for you.

Or if you struggle with making decisions and find yourself waiting to believe you know the exact right answer before any action is taken, then you've identified indecision as a major time bomb to address.

Mark your personal time bombs using the list below:

- Procrastination

- Indecision

- Distractions and Interruptions

- Stress and Overwhelm

- Relaxed Deadlines

Perfectionism

People Pleasing

Fatigue

Time Vs. Money

Developing Strategies

Now that you have identified the time bombs that most apply to you, it's time to move on to the next crucial step: developing strategies to overcome them.

The strategy that I suggest to be first is to call on your faith and ask God to help you with the journey you are embarking on to overcome these time bombs so you can be a greater steward to the time He has given you. When you pray and make your requests in His name, know that you are being helped.

Secondly, know that real change will also require a combination of mindset shifts and practical action steps on your part. Refer back to The Model we learned about in Chapter 6. This tool will give you clarity on the obstacles that are keeping you from getting the results you want.

As a reminder of The Model, we'll look at the circumstances, thoughts, feelings, actions, and results that are happening when we aren't using time like we want to.

For example, let's say you know that procrastination is one of your top three time bombs. You've specifically identified that when there are big house projects to be done, you tend to procrastinate. And let's say, for the sake of this example, that you're currently working on a project with your garage.

Your garage is a mess right now, but you're getting a new car and you really want to park it in the garage. There's just one problem, there's no room to park your new car in the garage. You have thoughts that you don't have time to organize the garage. You know how this generally goes, you see that this is exactly a time when the procrastination time bomb would disrupt your plans for a clean place to park your new car.

Using the model to work through this time bomb, we can see that the circumstance is the garage, particularly that there is no room in the garage to park a car. In this case, perhaps you are choosing to think that the garage is such a big project and you don't know where to begin. When you think about the garage in this way, those thoughts create a feeling in your body of overwhelm. It is from this feeling and emotion of overwhelm that drives you to take the action of procrastination.

So now you know why you're procrastinating. Along with those feelings, you come up with excuses not to clean the garage. You don't make preparations to organize or make the schedule out and decide when it's going to happen. Maybe you don't reach out for help for it to get done.

The example above using The Model is showing you what actions you're taking when you feel overwhelmed because you think it's such a big project and you don't know where to begin. But it's creating a clear result: you are no closer to making the time to clean out your garage. You're no closer to a clean garage to park your new car in.

Can you see how it all fits together? You have something that you want to get done, but the time bomb of procrastination is keeping you from utilizing your time to accomplish something that you want—like cleaning out the garage.

When you see it laid out like this, you can see that your thoughts and feelings about the garage are what actually keep you from taking the action you need so you can enjoy the result you want.

Use the template below to write it in your notebook and walk through one of your own examples using The Model.

Circumstance:

Thought:

Feeling:

Action:

Result:

To overcome this time bomb, we want to shift our thoughts to get ourselves in a better emotional space so we can try out some different actions.

Let's see what some of those possible thought and action shifts could look like using our garage example from before.

Here are a few suggestions for different thoughts that can begin to a shift procrastination:

- "I am determined to get this garage cleaned up."

- "Since the car is going to arrive next week, I'm committed to getting it done by this weekend no matter what."

- "I know where to start, I'll just start on this shelf in this corner."

- "I am going to get the help I need to be able to get it done on time."

If you were thinking the thoughts suggested above, or maybe you're just visualizing and thinking about how wonderful it would be to pull that car in a clean space, then you might feel motivated, inspired, determined, and committed to getting this task done. Then, the action wouldn't become procrastination. You would begin to take action toward getting the end goal of parking your car in a clean garage.

Let's take a look at another example. If you struggle with distractions and interruptions, you want to become aware of what those circumstances are like. Perhaps there's a phone call when you are sitting at your desk doing work. This is your circumstance.

The thought that naturally follows is, "Oh, I have to get that. I might be missing something." That's going to lead you to take the action of answering the phone and getting distracted from work as opposed to having that mindset to stay with what you said you were going to do. Considering your commitment to your task will lead to a decision of, "I will call them back later."

Review those places in your life that lend themselves to your top time bombs and use The Model to gain some awareness over how you can shift your thoughts, feelings, and actions.

After we have this new awareness of your time bombs, you can use The Model to investigate each of your top time bombs and take what they reveal to you so you can make the necessary mind and action shifts to start getting better time goal results.

In my life coaching practice, this is exactly how I help my clients focus and how to make those mental shifts, including accessing more tools and concepts that help you just like this model tool does. If you want more tools and help like this, send an email to danielle@daniellethienel.com or visit www.daniellethienel.com.

Having this awareness is the first key step to taking control of your time. It reveals exactly how you spend your time to get the results you currently have. Remember, dear moms, you have the power to reclaim your time and create a life that aligns with your values and aspirations. By identifying and overcoming your time bombs, you're taking a significant step towards achieving that balance and harmony you seek.

At this point in our time together, I want to express my admiration for your dedication and commitment to getting this far. You are going after a better life for yourself and your loved ones. If you embrace this journey of self-discovery and get curious about what is going on in your mind, your emotions, and your actions, then you will step into a future where Divine Time management becomes your reality. If you embrace this, you will love the results you get!

In the next chapter, I have a specific method I'd like to share with you about digital detoxing. This is a huge time bomb that plagues every mom in this day and age. The Model is a great start for help with digital distractions, but I have a few more tips to share with you...

CHAPTER 8

The Ultimate Digital
Detox Plan

Moms come to me all the time asking for help in managing their time and specifically around one of their main challenges: technology. I am commonly asked how to stop wasting time scrolling on a phone or binge-watching Netflix when there is so much to get done. These moms desire to be more present while setting an example for their children to be online less too.

We know it's important to prioritize quality time with our families, yet the constant presence of screens and technology can make it challenging to disconnect and engage with those we love.

This is especially true for children, who often spend hours each day watching TV, playing video games, and using smartphones or tablets. Involving your children in this digital detox plan can be a great way to spend quality time together and help them develop healthy habits around technology.

Here are a few strategies you can start to use today:

- **Schedule screen-free family time.** Set a specific time and duration for your family's screen-free activities.

- **Plan outdoor activities in advance.** Make a list of outdoor activities and schedule them in advance.

- **Create a list of hobbies and crafts.** Ask what activities your children enjoy and have those supplies on hand.

- **Model healthy tech habits.** Be mindful of your own screen time. Children learn by example.

Don't forget to involve your children in this process. It is possible to limit screen time and enjoy more quality time with those you love.

Handling FOMO

Digital FOMO (the fear of missing out) on social media can be a major obstacle to disconnecting from technology. This feeling arises when we see others sharing their experiences and accomplishments online and we fear that we're missing out on something important or exciting. As a result, we feel compelled to constantly check our social media feeds and notifications, even when it's not necessary.

When people decide to detox from phones, scrolling, and social media, they often worry about missing out on important events, news, or updates from friends and family. They may also worry that they'll feel disconnected from the world or fall behind on important information. These fears are understandable, but the truth is that they're often unfounded.

In reality, most of the information and content we see on social media is not essential to our lives or well-being. While it's important to stay informed and connected, we can do this through other means besides social media, such as reading news websites, attending community events, or engaging in conversations with friends and family.

It's also important to remember that social media presents a highly curated and often unrealistic version of people's lives. People tend to post only the best, most exciting parts of their lives online, creating a distorted view of reality. By taking a break from social media, we can gain a more realistic perspective on our own lives and relationships.

To ensure you don't miss out on important events or news, you could set specific times during the day to check news websites or receive updates from friends and family directly. You could also make plans with loved ones in advance to stay connected and engaged, rather than relying on social media to do so.

Digital FOMO can be a major obstacle to disconnecting from technology, but it's important to remember that most of the information and content we see on social media is not essential to our lives or well-being. By reframing our thinking about social media and finding other ways to stay informed and connected, we can overcome digital FOMO and create a healthier relationship with technology.

Life Without Social Media

With all that said, there is life beyond social media! Here are 5 ways to engage more in your life while lessening the time sabotage of electronic use.

1. **Make phone calls.** One of the simplest ways to stay connected with loved ones is by making phone calls. Schedule regular times to catch up and share news and updates.

2. **Send personal messages.** Instead of relying on social media to stay informed, send personal messages to friends and family via text, email, or instant messaging. This allows you to stay up-to-date without getting caught up in the endless scroll of social media feeds.

3. **Plan in-person meetings.** Make plans to meet up with friends and family in person. This could be anything from grabbing coffee or lunch to attending a local event or activity together.

4. **Join a club or group related to your interests or hobbies.** This is a great way to meet new people and stay connected with others who share your passions. Provide opportunities for in-person socializing and staying up-to-date with the latest news and events related to your interests.

5. **Attend community events in your area**, such as festivals, concerts, or charity events. This is a great way to meet new people, engage with your community, and stay informed about local news and happenings.

I used to struggle with the time I spent scrolling on the phone. I felt mad at myself at the end of the day for not getting done what I set out to accomplish. I also felt guilty for not being as present with my kids as I wanted to be. But when I created a plan and worked toward implementing its principles, I wasted less time and got more done each day.

The steps I've shared with you here were that plan. It worked and led me to a more divine experience of time management.

While handling the hold our technology often has on us is a huge step, it's only one piece of the Divine Time pie! In the next chapter, we will intentionally, deliberately, and consciously decide on a specific time management plan. This plan will determine how you're going to spend your time on your faith, yourself, your family, your home, and your work or vocation. This is where you will start to see the results that drove you to pick up this book in the first place!

It's time to stop wishing to start taking action towards making your reality one of Divine Time management. It's not how much time we have, it's about how we can create and control the time gifted to us.

CHAPTER 9

Our Relationship With Time

If time were a person, we would have the weirdest relationship with them.

We often relate to time as if we're mad at it. We say there's not enough of it, it went by too fast, or that we wish we had more of it but it's always against us.

We blame time. It's time's fault we are overwhelmed. We say, "Darn you, time. Why do you have to leave when I was just getting everything done?"

We feel victimized by time. We point out that our kids grow too fast. Our best years or qualities were robbed by the passage of time.

Except time simply exists. It just is. There are 24 hours in a day, 365 days in a year (except for the rare exceptions of daylight savings and leap year). So how can some of us feel like time is slipping through our fingers and others feel like there's plenty of it?

It all comes down to our relationship with time.

If you are blaming time, telling yourself that there's not enough time, or that you're mad at time, then it doesn't matter what kind of planner or reminder system we use—we will always have a bad relationship with time. But if you're willing to embrace different thoughts about time, you can drastically improve your experience of time.

Let's look at our experience of time like we would any other relationship. We deem a relationship "good" if we feel connected to the other person.

With our spouses, we feel connected when we have good conversations, fun outings, compliments, maybe gifts. We feel connected when we love each other and help each other be better people. When there is connection, there is joy. It makes you feel good. These connections are what sustain us through life. In times of trouble or grief, we lean on these connections.

Disconnection happens when we criticize our spouses or act negatively toward them. When we are disconnected from our spouses, we blame them for our heartache. Can you imagine what would happen if you spoke to your best friend in the same way you speak about time? If you blamed your friend for every missed opportunity or felt like you were a victim of their flippant friendship, that relationship would not last.

The way we speak about time greatly influences our relationship with time.

Another relationship comparison that can enhance our relationship with time is our connection with Christ. What are we thinking when we feel close to Him? When we have a good relationship with Christ, that comes after spending time with Him through reading scriptures or praying. We feel close to Christ when we participate in activities that keep us more aligned with Him.

If we extract lessons from this relationship, we can enhance our relationship with time. For example, reading, praying, and aligning ourselves with Christ show that we are prioritizing what is important in our day and our relationship with Him. So it is with time. When we organize what really matters, we stop feeling the need to blame time.

In fact, we notice this principle as we study Christ's life in the scriptures. He knew where He was needed and what His mission on earth was, and yet He did not hurry. Christ was never in a rush. From this, we can learn that when we prioritize our tasks and focus on what truly matters to us, our experience of time expands.

The way I implement this principle in my life is to start my day with a prayer. One of my favorites is, "Holy Spirit, come into my heart where you already abide. Please guide my thoughts, feelings, and actions today and may they align with God's will. Please make my crooked path straight."

I love that phrase, "Make my crooked path straight." The first thing I ask Him in the morning is to bless and order my time. Then, I allow things to unfold throughout my day without any control over them because I see Him as a companion.

He's the best roadmap for my day. If plans get canceled, I say, "Okay Lord, what's the best thing to do next?" I bring Him into my choices about how I spend my time. I do that with everything in my life. If you stop and bring Him into it, how can that not end up being better?

If you want to have a better relationship with time, or not always feel victimized at the mercy of time, bring the Lord as a companion throughout your day and the way you manage and speak to time.

I believe when you put God first, a natural order comes to your life. If you put God first, everything else falls into place. God has told us we can do all things through Him because He'll strengthen us. Apply that principle to your experience of time. God is with you.

No matter what relationship we're speaking of, our relationship with our spouse, best friend, kids, or our God on High—*every relationship exists within our mind.*

Let that sink in. Your relationship with your spouse is what it is because of what you think about it. Recall back to Chapter 6 when we discussed The Model. We experience circumstances and our feelings about those circumstances stem from the thoughts we have or the meaning we assign an experience.

I love the example of this principle in the context of Valentine's Day or Christmas. These are occasions where we typically exchange gifts with our spouses—holidays are circumstances. Whether they forget and don't get you anything or write you a love letter with roses are also just circumstances.

When it comes to relationships, we tend to look at what the other person is doing or not doing as an indicator of whether our relationship is good or not, but those things are just circumstances. Feeling connected or disconnected with our spouse comes from the meaning we assign the roses he gave us or the lack of a gift he showed up with.

If you think that your husband is the best companion for you and that you love how he loves you, and maybe he drives you nuts but you're here for it—that's why you have a good relationship. Not because of the flowers he brought you the other day or any romantic gestures. Your thoughts are what create that feeling of connection with him.

Shift back to thinking about your relationship with time. Do you judge time? Do you wish it was different than it is or think it forgets about you? Or do you think that time is lovely, that time is there for you?

When we feel stuck in a bad circumstance, we have two options: change the circumstance, or change our thoughts around our circumstance.

For example, let's say you blame your job as the reason you don't have any time for anything else in your life. You could change your circumstance and quit your job. With your freed up time, you would have time to spend with your kids or any of your other goals. There are obviously more factors to consider than just the time trade-off, but quitting that job is an option on the table. The alternative is to change your thoughts around your job and your time.

It's one or the other, and I honestly have no judgment which one you choose. I don't know what is best for you, but I do know you are capable of making that choice. But if you're tired and overwhelmed, there is a beautiful opportunity to decide what you would like to change so you can feel better about it. You can change your circumstances to have more time or change your thoughts about your circumstances and your experience of time.

One thing I want you to understand is that it is impossible to "waste" time. Read that again. It's impossible to "waste" time. You literally spend time how you spend it. That's just a fact, a circumstance.

The meaning we apply to how we spend our time is what we manage. If you want to feel better about how you're spending your time, make sure you feel good about yourself. That's what we're after here, feeling good about how you spend your time. We'll get to this in a later chapter, but self-care is a key factor in how you experience your time. Feeling good about yourself by actually taking care of yourself begets good feelings about your time. Self-care on a regular basis makes us happy, fills us up, and brings us joy.

Caring for yourself is going to create the feeling of more time, but the concept moms have now is that they need more time in order to do self-care. It's backwards. It's the opposite. There's a whole paradigm shift that needs to happen around the time we take to care for ourselves.

One simple thing you can start doing today as a way to shift your thoughts about time is to change how you approach your to-do list. Instead of putting all the tasks you need to do on a list, write your tasks as if you have already completed them and call it a "to-done" list. For example, don't write down, "go to the post office", instead phrase it as "mailed package" so it's in the form of already being done.

This literally gets your brain to think about the finished form and helps you focus on your gains and accomplishments. Practicing a "to-done" list will remind you to be proud of yourself and how you spend your time.

That's not natural for us. As humans, we tend to focus on our gaps and shortcomings, or what we didn't finish on our to-do list today. That feels terrible at the end of the day. Most moms cram their to-do list full of tasks and whatever they don't finish gets moved to the next day.

But what doesn't get put on our to-do list are things like: feeding and bathing the kids, tidying up the house, preparing meals, getting the kids off to school, etc. If moms were to start putting those daily tasks on their lists, they would see they're doing a heck of a lot more than they're giving themselves credit for!

If you start to look at what you are doing with your time that is important and that matters, what you are getting done and accomplished, then you're going to feel differently about how you're spending your time.

I will have accomplished my goal with this book if I can help you reconsider your relationship with time. Pay attention to the words you speak about time and shift your thoughts around your experience of time. You can feel connected to an expanse of time if you prioritize what is important by putting God first and inviting Him into your day. As you put first things first, prioritize taking care of yourself. As you feel better about yourself, it is easier to feel good about how you are spending your time. And if you experience a difficult circumstance, know that you can choose to either change your circumstance or your thoughts about your circumstance.

Give the "to-done" list a try and let me know what your experience is by emailing me at danielle@daniellethienel.com.

I promise that as you mindfully address your relationship with time, you can experience the calm that comes with knowing there is an abundance of time on your side.

CHAPTER 10

Create Your 3-Step Divine Time Saver Process

The three-step Divine Time Saver Process is something I developed to make Divine Time Management easier to conceptualize and live. This chapter will include each of the three steps to help you know exactly which steps to take so you can enjoy life by Divine Time.

Discern Your Life Mission

Our first step is a crucial one: discerning your life mission. This action brings us clarity that helps us not waste time on things that don't align with our values or who we want to be.

There is great benefit to discerning your own life's mission in regards to your current stage of motherhood. The mission of a young mother with several little ones will look different than the mom who has grown up kids with more independence. As you craft your mission statement, it's important to focus on where you are in life right now and what you want the driving factors of your time to be today and in your near future.

As a mom whose faith is very important to them, you have a unique set of values and beliefs that guide your actions and decisions. Your mission statement can help you align your goals and actions with your faith and values so you can live a more purposeful and fulfilling life. That will change as you grow and change as your children grow and change, so keeping the focus on your goals now will enhance your relationship with your time with what's going on today.

The concept of mission statements dates back to the Middle Ages when monasteries would use them to define their purpose and values. Today, mission statements are commonly used in businesses and organizations, but they can also be helpful for moms and families who want to clarify their goals and priorities.

The most common reasons that organizations today use them translate beautifully to helping us save time.

These are reasons include:

1. A mission statement provides direction and focus for what you stand for.

2. A mission statement lays out what you hope to achieve and expresses the values that you hold dear.

3. A mission statement helps us align our decision-making and fosters accountability to carry those choices out daily.

I encourage you to have a mission statement for these very same reasons. After all, you and your family are also sort of an organization, and most of the time it's the mom who is the CEO. Generally speaking, we are the ones running the show and keeping it all going. You will save yourself time when you are a mom who has direction and focus. Crafting a mission statement will give you clarity of purpose and have you showing up using your guiding principles, which are the values we hold as members of the Catholic faith or any other Christian faith you may hold.

Our principles and values represent what we stand for, what we hope to achieve, and what values we hold most dear. Having a personal mission statement will inspire and motivate us as we're working towards our goals.

Living mindful of your mission statement can also help you attract other moms who share the same values and beliefs. For example, let's say that it's part of your personal mission to stay connected to other moms who have children with similar ages of yours. We could be inspired and motivated to start our own moms group or Bible study if connecting with other moms is laid out as part of your personal mission at this stage of life.

A personal mission statement can also keep us out of what I like to call the "compare and despair." What I mean is that you and your family have needs that are unique and compelling to you and what's important to you, and that doesn't look the same as all the others that you may be seeing around.

This statement can help you stay focused on what will serve your family in the long run. When it comes to what other moms are doing with their time (perhaps from what you see on social media) you can start to use your time in a way that moves you towards what those other moms are doing and pull you away from the things you want to do when you're not stuck in the comparison trap.

Maybe you see other moms traveling a lot because their kids are older, or perhaps you see other moms who get help and support from nearby family and you don't experience that. These experiences can pull focus from how you want to show up as a mom and, instead, can influence you to try and seek out another mom's path.

A mission statement helps you keep focus on your own experiences and your own path. It helps you know what best supports your journey during this stage of your family's life.

You can use your mission to help you make choices that align with your family's core values and it can lead you to greater consistency across different areas of how you use your time.

Here's another example I've seen from a few of my coaching clients. If you are deciding to homeschool, you'll have to evaluate the time necessary to carry out this decision and put it up against your mission statement. By comparing the choice to your mission statement, acting as a baseline, you can see if that decision aligns with your overall goals for your family.

If your current mission includes having plenty of time to freely come and go to travel places a lot as a family, you might be better able to strongly decide that homeschooling is the right choice for you because of the schedule freedom it allows where traditional school adheres to a more strict calendar.

Overall, one of the most effective foundational tools for time management is creating a personal mission statement. It will help you articulate your purpose for your current stage of motherhood, keep you on track to achieve your goals in a meaningful way. Not only that, but including your faith life values mean that you would carry out this mission in a divine way.

Here are a few examples of Motherhood Mission Statements:

> Example #1: From a stay-at-home mom with young children.
>
> *To nourish and nurture my family through intentional, faith-centered mothering, while cultivating a loving, Christ-centered home*

environment that fosters spiritual growth and the development of strong moral character.

Example #2: from a mom with a mix of school-aged children and teenagers.

To guide my children towards a life rooted in faith, love, and service while maintaining open communication, fostering self-discovery, and celebrating each child's unique talents so they can become the individuals God created them to be.

Example #3: from a working mom who owns a small business.

To balance my roles as a loving mother and a devoted business owner, prioritizing quality time with my family while using my God-given talents to serve others and setting an example of perseverance, integrity, and faith in action for my children.

Can you see how these statements focus on the overall goal for these women's lives? They cite their faith values and incorporate how that looks within their current role.

My mission statement served as a guiding light when I was presented with two competing opportunities.

I had been asked to lead a one-day retreat for several parishes in a state far away – and of course I said yes! Speaking engagements are something I always love to do because connecting with people and sharing my life coaching tools and strategies brings me much joy and much needed knowledge to others. I booked my flight and began to plan my presentation for the trip.

However, not too long after I made this decision, I learned that the same day would be a Mother/Son event at my son's school. At the time this event took place, he was a senior in High School. This would be the last opportunity for this type of event.

At first there was inner turmoil that arose because I needed to choose between two events I very much wanted to attend, but because my current mom mission statement includes being present for my children's important events during this last year before college, I was able to know that following this Divine Time step would bring me the most peace and be the best use of my time.

Though it wasn't easy, following my mission statement allowed me to choose from a place of purpose and gave me clarity. You too, will find having a mom mission statement to be a most helpful tool to keep from staying stuck or questioning your next moves.

Now it's your turn! As you complete this next section in the space below or in your own notebook, keep in mind that you want your statement to be what's most important to you, not a straight copy from one of the examples above. Keep it short and simple, easy enough to memorize. And last, make sure it is relevant to your current stage of motherhood.

- Step 1: Introduction. Details about your state in life. *Example: I'm Danielle, a Catholic mom in her forties and mom of three teenagers.*

- Step 2: Core Values. List the core values and beliefs that are most important to you as a mom. *Example: Faith, love, kindness, impact, balance and joy, service, loyalty, commitment, and patience.*

- Step 3: Identify your goals and priorities. *Example: I will prioritize time with God each day, take great care of myself mentally and physically, and serve my clients as a channel of peace in God's will.*

- Step 4: Add specific, measurable, actionable, relevant, and time-bound details. *Example: I want to have prepared for college tuition by June and served 100 moms through my coaching practice by the end of the year.*

- Step 5: Put it all together! Form your personal mission statement below. *Example: As a devoted Catholic wife and mother, I embrace Christ's teachings while strengthening my marriage, caring for my parents, guiding my children, and prioritizing my own health. In God's plan, I use my coaching business to serve the world and help moms find balance. I commit to being a good steward of my finances, prioritizing tithing and my children's education. In all aspects, I put God first, aligning my actions with His divine guidance.*

Craft your mission statement in your journal or somewhere you can easily access it for reference.

After you finalize your mission statement, commit it to memory. Regularly remind yourself of your mission statement and use it as a guiding principle in your daily life.

As a last note on mission statements, an integral part of your success to carry out The Divine Time Solution will depend on reviewing and revising your statement. Time does pass and before you know it, you'll be in a different stage of motherhood. As your life changes and evolves, your mission statement may need to be reviewed and updated to reflect your current priorities and goals. This reevaluation process will help guide your decisions to stay on track with your time priorities.

Take A Time Audit

I highly encourage you to slow down and take your time with this section. A time audit could feel like a tedious task to you at the moment but it will eventually help you save a bunch of time and affect your future in such a positive way. This is a short-term discomfort for long-term gain and an eyeopener to many of you who have just been putting your head down and getting done what you can each day.

When you conduct a time audit, you're forced to slow down and bring a new level of consciousness to your life that may not have been there before. I know you'll be fascinated at how much time there really is available to you from what you discover doing this assignment.

We'll then use your findings in the next section to evaluate where you could make some shifts in your schedule. That will then help you tremendously.

Think of a time audit similar to how doctors or nutritionists ask us to keep track of our food intake when we're trying to uplevel our physical health.

Before we dive in, let's define what a time audit actually is. Our trusty friend Google says, "A time audit is an examination of how you're spending your time so that you can make more intentional choices with the minutes and hours in your days." It involves documenting yourself for a period of time, ideally a week, but I'm asking you to take a minimum of three to five days.

Either way, you'll log your activities and the amount of time you spend on each of them. I'm also interested in how you feel when you do each of these activities because this plays a greater role in the outcome of how you spend your time—more than you may have thought.

The time audit is important because it's an honest look at your current time management habits and routines. Now, let me insert a caveat here. Once you see how much time you might be "wasting" or see a list of things that don't line up with your mission at the moment, I do not want you to judge yourself. Please don't beat yourself up mentally for not doing something about it before now or using your results as an excuse to quit or stop because you believe you can't change. This negative self talk will not serve your time goals or provide any benefit at all.

This is where I want you to remember The Model tool we talked about in Chapter 6. Your thoughts are important to the success of your results. We want your thoughts focused toward what is possible for you, not the defeated feeling that arises from how you handled your time in the past.

Depending on what you find from the audit, it might reveal that you only need a few tweaks and minor adjustments. Or perhaps you'll feel motivated to do an entire overhaul of your schedule. Either way, a time audit will instill a sense of empowerment because you are taking charge of your time—and therefore your life.

There are three major benefits that often result from conducting a time audit.

One, you'll identify areas where you're wasting time so you'll know how to then prioritize differently going forward.

Two, you'll see improvements in your level of productivity and a reduction in the amount of stress you feel because you'll be empowered by the possibility to take control of your time.

And three, after your time audit is complete, you'll have a clear snapshot of where you're currently directing your time, energy, and effort. You'll know if your current habits contribute to your mission and goals. And if they don't, then with that information (and the tools you learn in this book!) you'll be able to change that.

Here is the process you'll follow while completing your time audit.

1) Pick your audit days that will fall in a typical or normal type of week for you and your family. Unforeseen circumstances can arise

THE DIVINE TIME SOLUTION

that you weren't expecting and shifts may need to be made because stuff comes up. The goal here is to find out what you're doing on an ordinary day, not a vacation week or when you're hosting out of town guests.

2) Take note of every activity you do throughout the day from waking up to going to bed. Write it all down. You can use your own journal or a couple of pieces of paper.

   a) Use your phone or other device to set an alarm to remind you when it's time to write down all the things you've done in that timeframe. You can set your alarm for every hour or thirty minutes as needed. Pick an amount of time that will allow you to recall the details of what you just spent your time on.

   b) Keep this record for the whole day, each day of the audit. Write any additional details about the tasks you did such as where you were, who you were with, how you felt during that time, if you noticed any particular time bombs that showed up for you, etc.

Continue this pattern for 3–7 days, knowing that each additional day you choose to track will give you a clearer picture of how you spend your time overall.

Start now. Even as you keep reading, you can set an alarm. (And wouldn't 'reading' be a pretty great activity to have on your time audit?)

After your time audit is complete, you'll notice a new level of consciousness around how you spend your time. The next section of this chapter is intended to be completed after you are finished with your audit. Feel free to read ahead now, but come back around to this section when your audit is finished.

Decide What to Keep and What to Let Go

Now it's time to put all that hard work of tracking your activities from the time audit to further use. In this section, you'll make decisions about how you choose to spend your time and what you would like to spend less time on—or stop certain activities altogether.

With a clear picture of how you spend your time, ask yourself to answer the following important questions to identify where you're wasting time and where you can be more efficient. Maybe you noticed you spent more time than you want scrolling through social media or watching television. Or perhaps you see that each day, your morning routine took more time than necessary and it's a place in your day you've been wanting to streamline and get the kids ready for school more efficiently.

Did you have any time for yourself on a daily basis?

Did the activities you complete include any prayerful blocks of times or silent moments?

Were there any tasks that don't fit with your mission statement you wrote in section 1 of this chapter?

See, by making small adjustments to your daily routine, you can save yourself valuable time. And if you made note of the things that elevated your stress levels, you can evaluate if they are necessary requirements for your life at the moment, or you can make a plan to reduce the stress going forward from your daily activities. (And a life coach is a perfect partner to help you work through this!)

Become mindful and notate any time wasting activities you are engaging in, such as social media, tv, or phone calls that could have waited.

Were there any moments where you felt you could have been more productive or efficient?

Where are the places you found yourself making excuses to avoid doing the task?

Where can you cut back on time wasting activities or be more efficient?

What were the moments where you had to shift priorities or adjust your schedule?

Look over everything you tracked and discover any patterns or trends—that's where the real gold can be buried. Decide what adjustments you can make to your overall schedule or routine to better prioritize your time and increase efficiency. With these insights, you now can make some strong decisions.

What do you want to stop doing altogether?

What do you want to consciously decide to do less of?

What doesn't currently align with your mission and is better suited for a later time in your mom-life journey?

What do you want to trade-out doing instead?

Continue to audit every so often to find where you can save yourself time and use it more wisely for the life you want to live, and with your new deeper conviction of living life by Divine Time. See what you can let go of and what you want to keep in your schedule on purpose.

PART 3

Your Personalized Divine Time Life Plan

CHAPTER 11

The 5 Pillars You Want to Spend Your Time On

In this chapter, I want to hone in on the five pillars of things we moms want to make time for. This will prepare you to work through your very own personalized Divine Time plan for this stage of your life as well as the tools you will need to keep balance in your daily life.

After conducting a survey with over 600 busy Catholic moms answering the questions of what they most wanted to have more time for, I was able to distill their answers into what I use as my five pillars. These essential pillars will become the foundation for a balanced and fulfilling life as a mom.

Make Time For Faith

The first pillar to establish in your Divine Time plan is to make time for your faith. Being a member of the Catholic Church is my guiding light in my life, yet for us moms of faith, our faith practices often take a backseat to the demands of our busy schedules.

Many moms have shared with me that they struggle to make time for their faith. They feel guilty about not attending mass regularly, not setting aside quiet moments for prayer, or not participating in certain spiritual activities.

Before we move on, I want to tell you that I understand how guilty you can feel when you don't have enough time for your faith. Whether you've had a significant life event, like welcoming home a new baby, or life simply got out of hand, it can feel like you want to go all in to fix the deficit of faith. It can seem like you need a major overhaul, but that's not the case.

Any progress is good progress. Five minutes a day will suffice. You could do a decade, or ten beads on the Rosary. Perhaps you set an alarm on your phone to say an Our Father, Hail Mary, or a Glory Be.

If you feel hopeless about the time spent on your faith, a little is enough. Sometimes, our brain tells us we have to go the full monty, that we need seven hours with Christ each week. That would be great, but if you're starting at zero, how amazing would it feel to have 2 or 3 hours with Christ in a week?

I promise that God knows what is going on in your life. He knows what you're juggling. Any progress in attention or focus is good for you and is enough. Your effort doesn't need to be enormous.

At this first stage in creating your Divine Time plan, what goals would you like to set around making time for your faith? Would you like to go to church each week, spend time in adoration, or have a dedicated study hour by yourself?

Some ideas from other moms include:

- Time to pray before they get their kids up in the morning

- Saying the Rosary more

- Participating in a Bible Study group or spiritual retreat

Now that you have what it takes to be in control of your time through what I've laid out in this book, it's time for you to get specific on what particular faith activities you want to make time for.

At the time of this writing, there is an app I use called Hallow. It helps me fit in time for my faith because it has already curated daily words of the gospel or prayers.

Imagine the joy and peace you'll experience when you are prioritizing your faith and making time for these activities that up until now have been more elusive for you.

I can't think of a better way to order your life than making time to connect with Christ in some way, however big or small, that works for your stage of motherhood. I truly believe when you do this one step, all the other categories get divinely blessed too.

Make Time For You

So the second pillar is making time for you, moms. It's crucial to remember that you deserve time for self-care and personal growth. It's crucial and without it, you cannot be the effective and efficient mom you want to be. It's common for us to neglect our own needs while taking care of everyone else. We love our family so much and want to serve them well, but it often overshadows our own human needs that are necessary to function at our best.

Have you found yourself saying, "I don't have time for a hobby," or "I can't remember the last time I did something just for me?"

Well, I've heard from many moms who dream of reading a book for pleasure, taking a nap in the day, or simply taking a relaxing bubble bath without someone yelling for their mama. These are all things you can include in your personalized plan.

One thing I want to emphasize about self-care is that it's not a one-size-fits-all approach. My favorite approach to use is to ask yourself, "What sounds fun or loving to do for myself today?"

After the events in Chapter 4 where I got sick, quit my job, and reevaluated the way I was spending my time, I began with this question. The first answer was time in prayer, my own personal time with Christ each morning. I also found that prioritizing my health through exercise made me happy, and I also began reaching out and connecting with friends. These moments of self-care filled my cup in ways I couldn't have anticipated beforehand.

As I prioritized my own 'me time,' I found that I showed up as the mom and woman I wanted to be. I was filled with more patience and foresight as I dealt with my children, spouse, and others in my community. While that might seem surprising and certainly backwards than we typically learn from a societal standpoint—which says to serve others before we think of ourselves—the principle here is crucial.

Imagine that you are a bucket. When you are in use, or helping others, you can develop cracks and holes if you don't take care of yourself. Even if you are able to function with cracks in your sides, it causes more damage than good because the water leaks out of the side, draining you.

Like the bucket, if you are giving yourself to others, even in good ways, while you are cracking and developing holes, you will cause more damage to yourself. This is where moms can burnout and feel like they are only surviving from day to day.

Instead, prioritizing time to yourself each day to make yourself happy plugs those holes and fills those cracks, allowing you to show up completely to the relationships and areas you contribute to.

This follows the principle of Divine Order, which goes hand-in-hand with Divine Time. The Divine Order dictates that God comes first. Then, in order of importance and focus, is your own self, your spouse, your children, your extended family, your community, and lastly your work. Notice how, in the Divine Order, you come before your spouse and your children? It is because you can only fully show up as a wife and mother after you take care of yourself as an individual.

We often operate in the opposite way. We tell ourselves that we can only have time to ourselves after we finish our chores for the day, care for our children, and perhaps if we have any extra time, we can care for ourselves. Some moms prioritize their 'me-time' during a young child's nap time or other naturally calmer moments in the day. But what happens when your young child refuses to nap or gets sick and needs extra attention during those calm moments? Cracks and holes start to form in your bucket, mama.

One of the greatest lessons I have learned is this principle of Divine Order. Pouring attention into myself before others allows me to show up and live the life I want to live. I am the wife, mom, and woman of Christ I want to be because I prioritize repairing my bucket.

I ask that you focus on this pillar of making time for yourself and take the steps to have it reflect in your schedule. Remember to keep in mind your current mission and stage of motherhood and know that in different stages it may be quicker, more bite-sized kind of self-care than say what I have time for these days as a mom of college-aged children.

Overall, I stress the importance of giving yourself some "Me time." Give yourself time to recharge your batteries. Take exquisite care of yourself. You can be the mom and wife God created you to be.

Make Time For Family

We now move on to our third pillar, which is to make time for family. Our families are our greatest joy. However, in the hustle and bustle of daily life, it's easy to lose sight of the precious moments we share with our loved ones.

How often have you caught yourself saying, "I wish I had more quality time with my children," or "I feel disconnected from my spouse?"

My clients express to me their desire to have regular family dinners, engage in meaningful conversations with their children, plan outings together, or go on a vacation to strengthen family bonds. In fact, what I hear most often from busy moms is that they wish they had more one-on-one time with each of their children. Are any of these examples resonating with you?

If you are a mom who wants to focus on having more time with your family, I encourage you to get more specific about what that looks like. Ask yourself what you would do with your family if you had an extra hour each day. Get into the details as you plan: what are you doing? Who is involved? What conversations are you having?

A specific goal is much easier to accomplish than a half-formed idea. For example, if you want more time with your teenager — I've been there! — then perhaps you set a goal for a ten-minute conversation on the way to band practice while the two of you are alone in the car. The specificity of this goal allows you to check the box, so to speak, and go to bed knowing you took time to connect with your child that day. Having a specific target to work toward can help ease the guilt we sometimes feel.

A common thought error we fall into is the overall comparison to other families and mothers. We can sometimes feel guilty when our family time doesn't look like the family time we see others partake in, especially if we find ourselves frequently on social media (feel free to revisit Chapter 8 if this resonates with you).

Just as they did when crafting our mission statements, the different stages of motherhood will affect the goals you set for your family time. When I was in high school, I spent my evenings in dance class and studying for my career in ballet. During this stage of my mother's life, she kept a dinner plate warming in the oven for me instead of trying to wrangle family dinners with an impossible schedule. This system worked for my family when I was a teenager.

When your kids are young, it can sometimes feel like your entire existence is spent in this pillar of family time, or particularly "kid time." When those children grow up, it can feel like suddenly everyone is going in their own different directions. Purely by virtue of the change in your stage of motherhood, you can feel like things are not going as well with your family because it no longer looks the same as it did when your kids were little. Time with your spouse and your kids will change with each season of motherhood. Do what you can to let go of any judgements on your performance based on other motherhood stages that do not apply to you.

Being intentional about the specific ways you want to engage with your family can help you create lasting memories and foster deeper connections with the people you love the most. Choose specific goals based on your stage of motherhood and, as it was with our pillar of faith, know that the effort of a five-minute conversation or a quick hug can still contribute to your connection with those you love.

Make Time For Home

The fourth pillar is making time for your home. As moms, we are the heart of our homes. However, maintaining a tidy and organized household can often feel like an impossible task and something we feel a lack of time for.

Do you find yourself saying, "I can never keep up with the laundry." Or, "My home feels chaotic and cluttered?" Or even, "I wish I felt better about the state of my home"?

I've heard from many moms, who long for a clean and peaceful living environment, how they wish to establish cleaning routines, declutter their spaces, or create a welcoming atmosphere for their families but find it a challenge to get there. We ultimately want a place that feels good and comfortable for ourselves and our families—and we will always spend some portion of our time cleaning, decorating, and maintaining our home.

When noticing you want to spend some time on your home, first decide what to focus on in relation to your home, start with where you are today. What is your home situation? From there, like we have discussed in other sections, get clear about the goals you have for your current home while taking into consideration your current circumstances. Do you want less clutter? Are you trying to establish a consistent laundry routine? Do you want to update the decorations?

In my coaching career, I have worked with countless busy moms who yearn for a more organized home so they can enjoy a more peaceful space. To help you make any time you spend here more fruitful, I'd like to share with you my approach to a sustainable change that you can incorporate into your everyday life. This approach includes three steps to transform your home from chaos to calm.

#1 - Why is home organization important to you? Stated differently, what is the reason that compels you, specifically, to focus on your home? This is also known as your "why" in many spaces. Knowing your own personal reason for home organization is crucial because it will serve as your beacon. Make sure you are honest with yourself to choose a reason that feels aligned with your personal heart's desire and not one driven by what you think you *should* want or pick a reason because you think others/ society expects it.

#2 - A decluttered home starts with a decluttered mind. Often, we create clutter because of thoughts we have about our possessions like sentimentality or anxiety about needing an object for the future. Your emotional state can either perpetuate clutter or stem from it. Focus on positive thoughts surrounding your possessions like, "While this was a gift, it doesn't serve a purpose in my life." These positive thoughts will allow you to let go of the clutter and bring a feeling of satisfaction as you maintain an organized home.

#3 - Use these three key decision-making questions when choosing what to keep and what to let go of as you transform your home into the space you want most. Remember, the goal is not minimalism or a bare house. (Unless that's something you want to experience!) This process is all about curating your possessions to optimize your life experience.

> First: "Does it serve my life to keep this item?" Is it relevant to your current lifestyle? Does it bring you joy or enhance your well-being? If the answer is yes, keep the item. If the answer is 'no,' then it's time to let it go. Follow this same procedure with the next two questions as well.

> Second: "Do I even like or truly want this object?" It's not uncommon to hold on to items out of obligation, guilt, or even habit rather than a genuine love for them.

> Third: "Is this item current or outdated?" Another way to ask this question is to ask yourself, is this an item I would buy again? If you wouldn't buy it again, perhaps it is time to let it go.

As you let go of any items, remember that while it may not be valuable to you, it could be valuable to someone else. Make space for what matters and let go of what doesn't. I also recommend you don't tackle your entire home in one day. Consider taking one room or space at a time.

As you are mindful about your mental space, you will notice an improvement in organization in your physical space.

Make Time For Work

Lastly, the fifth pillar is making time for your work. We must recognize the importance of our work, job, career, business or vocation, whatever name suits you best. Even if you're someone whose work involves volunteering, this would be the category where that goes.

Whatever you are naming this important part of ourselves and whether it entails you work outside the home in a job or within your home raising your children, it's vital you take control over what your time spent here looks like. It is also important that you find fulfillment and purpose—not only in what you do, but also in the amount of time used to carry it out.

Have you found yourself saying, "I feel overwhelmed by my workload," or "I'm not able to do X, Y, or Z for the house or myself because of my career?"

You are one human being with limited time and energy. This can be difficult to remember when you're trying to juggle everything at once! I often remind my coaching clients that when you say yes to one thing, you're also simultaneously saying no to another. What you say yes to and what your work time looks like will likely morph and change through the different stages of motherhood.

Whatever you choose, and like we've mentioned in other sections, know the reason you are making that choice. If you choose to work outside of the home because of a compelling financial reason, then great! If you choose to be a stay at home mom because of an inner conviction, fantastic. Sometimes mamas choose a vocation because it fills them up or sets an example for their children. Your reasons are your own and are absolutely valid. Identify those reasons for yourself in terms of your work life but then also remember to own and take responsibility for the choices you make in your mind. Ultimately, your thinking about your work will be the reason you feel good or not about your work life experience.

My mom clients have shared their desires to pursue their passions, explore new career opportunities, and find balance between work and family life. Divine Time in this pillar means understanding your reasons behind your choices, making choices aligned with those reasons, and knowing that when you say yes to one activity, you say no to another. When you take ownership of the time you spend in this pillar, are more mindful of how you implement this pillar in your life, and are intentional about the choices you make internally about your work life, you will create a fulfilling experience for yourself here.

Creating Your Own Plan With the 5 Pillars

So now that we've identified these five pillars, it's time for you to decide what goals you have within these five pillars that you currently aren't hitting but now want to start making progress in and what they are specifically for you.

My favorite way to craft this plan is to open a spreadsheet on my computer and label columns with the questions I'll share below. You can do this however you wish, though I encourage you to write it down or record it in some way that allows you to check-in regularly and make adjustments as necessary.

1) Take each pillar one at a time:

   a) Faith

   b) Self

   c) Family

   d) Home

   e) Work/Profession

2) For each pillar, consider each prompt:

   a) What I want to spend my time doing that I am not currently doing

   b) What specifically would that look like for me?

   c) Obstacles/time bombs currently in the way

   d) Strategies to put into place to overcome Time Bombs

   e) Is this pillar a high or low priority for my current stage of motherhood?

Remember, making intentional choices and committing to making adjustments will be the key to your decisions going forward.

When you have more time for your faith, even dedicating a few minutes each day to connect with your faith can have a profound impact on your time. Enjoying dedicated time to yourself on a regular basis, prioritizing quality family moments together, implementing practical strategies to keep your living space organized, integrating your professional and personal responsibilities in an enriching way—that is when you are living by Divine Time. That is when you have control over your time. That is when you will feel like you are living a life of purpose and peace.

Over the years of life coaching women, I have noticed a particular resistance to the notion of self-care and taking time to ourselves. Even if it's something we know we need to do, it's often the first thing to fall to the bottom of the to-do list (and perpetually pushed to tomorrow). The next chapter will hopefully convince you of the sacred importance, and the profound benefits, that await when taking care of your best asset as a divine mother: yourself.

CHAPTER 12

Divine Time and Self-Care

Self-care is often associated with the notion of being selfish or putting oneself first. However, the truth is that self-care is far from being selfish.

In fact, prioritizing self-care is crucial for overall health and well-being, especially for moms who often put the needs of their family and loved ones before their own.

Let's take a look at the true definition of 'selfish.' Being selfish means putting one's own interests or needs above the interests or needs of others without regard for their feelings or well-being.

Self-care, on the other hand, is about taking care of oneself so that they can show up as their best self for others. This means taking the time to rest, recharge, and rejuvenate, so that moms can better support and care for their families.

When moms put themselves first, it's not taking away from their family or loved ones, but instead, it's the opposite. By prioritizing self-care, moms can better meet the needs of their family and loved ones. When moms are feeling their best, they are better equipped to handle the demands and stressors of daily life, which ultimately benefits everyone in the family.

Moreover, it's important to note that the Divine order of God is to put Him first, followed by yourself, then your spouse, kids, other family/community, job, and then things. This order reflects the importance of taking care of ourselves so that we can better serve others. When we prioritize our own self care, we are better equipped to serve God and others.

Additionally, self-care is not just about taking care of oneself physically, but also mentally, emotionally, and spiritually. It's about finding activities and practices that bring joy and peace to one's life. This can include things like meditation, exercise, spending time in nature, reading a book, or even taking a nap.

So let this settle into your soul mama—it's important that you understand that self-care is not selfish, but rather an essential part of taking care of yourself so that you can show up as your best self for others.

One of my favorite phrases to date has become my signature line in coaching sessions, "You're not a robot, mama."

"Me time" is an important part of being a fully-functioning human being, let alone a human being that cares for others. And because we are not robots and are, in fact, human—we have limits to both our energy and time.

Unlike a robot, yes, we have human limits. And it's not just necessary for us to enforce these limits, but it's sacred that we do. It's a sacred call that we honor our "me time."

Machines are designed to perform tasks without rest. Without the need for sleep or rejuvenation or even joy. Robots work tirelessly. They work efficiently. But they do so without complaint.

And here's the catch: you, mama, are not a robot. Unlike these machines, we are beautifully human. We're crafted by God with care and intention, and included in this is the need for rest and renewal.

Think about it. Even in the very design of our world, there is a rhythm. Day turns to night. Seasons change. All living things grow, rest, and rejuvenate in cycles. It's a divine reminder that rest is not only natural, but it's necessary. It's necessary for us as humans. And that is how, as moms, we become the best version of ourselves—and to be more efficient ourselves is to recall that it's vital that we have these cycles of growth, rest, rejuvenation.

Yet, as busy moms, we often push this need aside. We pack our schedules, we juggle a whole bunch of responsibilities, and we even pride ourselves in our ability to keep going despite the human need to rest.

But at what cost? Just as a candle flickers out without wax, we can burnout without taking the time to replenish ourselves.

Let's talk about redefining the time we take for ourselves. I feel incredibly passionate about helping moms redefine "me time" for themselves and to really open themselves up to seeing how all that they want to accomplish in their life is really an easier, more straight path when you reorder your life that makes "me time" a priority.

To be clear, it's not just an hour stolen for a spa visit or a quick coffee alone. Those are wonderful, don't get me wrong. I totally encourage them, but it's about acknowledging your human need for rest, for stillness, silence, and for moments of doing absolutely nothing without guilt.

I know many of you are reading that and thinking, "Yeah, that's really hard for me. Doing absolutely nothing and not feeling guilty for it. Sure thing, Danielle."

Can you be bored for just 15 minutes? How about 30 minutes? I know that might be difficult for you, but if you redefine it and you look at that rest, quiet, and moments of stillness without guilt, that will help you in the long run.

Imagine if a robot tried to perform its tasks beyond its programming or even without maintenance. It would malfunction. It would break down eventually. And in a way, we have our programming too. That programming is, we have a need for sleep, we have a need for peace, for moments of joy, and ones that are actually not tied to our roles as mothers or partners or even professionals.

Let that sink in for a second. This need for sleep, peace, moments of joy, and connection with our Creator is part of your programming as a human. Yes, we want to find them in our professional life, in our motherhood, and with our relationship with our spouses, but we also need to find it outside of those roles. That's where "me time" comes in. It's your maintenance that allows you to continue in your daily tasks as a mother.

Me time is how you recharge your batteries, not just physically, but emotionally and spiritually. And I know that coaching is for sure mental me time. It also fills me up emotionally, spiritually and even leads to better physical well being too. But whether it's reading a book for you, sitting quietly in prayer time, taking a walk, or simply sitting with your thoughts, maybe journaling, these moments are your right. They're your necessity.

I want to challenge you to look at your week ahead. Where can you schedule your me time? I mean actually schedule it. As you would any important meeting. Pull out a pen and label it on the calendar. Set it as an event or task in your phone and include reminders—because this truly matters, mamas. I want you to see this time as non-negotiable.

I also don't want you to look at it as having to give up something in order to have it. I want you to look at having me time as what is going to actually help every other aspect of your life. It is a sacred appointment with yourself, and one that benefits you and your family greatly.

This appointment is a declaration that you're human and not a machine. It's a declaration that your needs matter and that you need maintenance and rest.

Remember in the grand design that even God rested on the seventh day. He set a divine example for us, signaling the importance of rest and reflection.

Your me time is not a luxury as much as your brain has been taught to think that it is. It's not. It's a fundamental part of your design.

You are not a robot. You are wonderfully complex. You are a divinely created being who deserves moments of rest and renewal. I want you to honor this design by embracing your need and desire for more me time.

I'm willing to bet that you, reading this book right now, could use that reminder. I'm also willing to bet that you know another mom out there who is lacking in rest and rejuvenation, who is taking on too much, saying yes to everything, and juggling too much. I'm willing to bet that you can see the burn-out and overwhelm in other moms present in your circles. Please pass this phrase on to them—or even this book!

Schedule that sacred appointment with yourself, my not-a-robot-mama. It will pave the way to a more calm, connected, and confident tomorrow.

As in all things, we strive for a balanced life. Balance is not achieved by shirking one area of our lives. All five pillars need to be present, addressed, and balanced within the demands of our current stage of motherhood as well as tested against our personal mission statements.

CHAPTER 13

Finding the Balance
in Your Life

In the Divine Time plan we created in Chapter 10, we outlined several goals across multiple pillars of life. While it sets you up for an efficient and effective use of your time, sometimes having multiple goals at the same time can feel overwhelming.

This chapter is all about how you find balance within the goals you created. Balance is how you stay focused within your areas of faith, self, family, home, and work. It's essential to stay focused and avoid the trap that I see many moms fall into, a pitfall that keeps you out of balance—the "all or nothing" mindset.

Finding balance means making some progress in each of the areas, even if it's just a little. And this balance comes from what you are thinking about yourself, your progress, and your results.

Think back to Chapter 6 where we discussed The Model. Balance is a feeling we experience, so we know from The Model that feeling balanced comes from our thoughts and not from our circumstances outside of us. And if you are feeling balanced, you will take action from there and create amazing results.

I highly recommend the tool of constraint, which guides you to pick one of the high priority activities and implement them one at a time. Add as you can and focus on no more than three to five at one time, depending on how strenuous those goals are. This will ensure that your time and energy are allocated effectively, allowing you to make consistent strides in your goals while maintaining a sense of balance.

It's common for all of us to fall into this all or nothing trap, believing that unless we can dedicate significant time and effort to each pillar, then we're not making progress. It's a seductive thought that actually keeps us from making progress altogether.

Let me tell you a secret: even small steps count! They add up. Instead of waiting for the perfect conditions or an abundance of free time available, focus on what you can do in the present moment. Do something, anything, and then celebrate the (small) victories and recognize that every effort you make, no matter how small, contributes to a more balanced life.

Building momentum is key to maintaining a balanced life plan. When you consistently make progress in each pillar, it creates a positive mindset and reinforces the belief that you are actively working towards your goals and that you are doing it; you are using your time divinely along your journey to find balance.

You will encounter challenges that make it difficult for you to stay on track, and it's important to be prepared and develop strategies to overcome these obstacles. As you carry out your personalized divine time plan, remember to look for ways to delegate and receive help. I also encourage you to check on whether you are setting realistic expectations for yourself.

I'm always reminding my life coaching clients that we are only one human being caring for several other human beings, and we have a limited resource of time and energy to spend each day.

If you encounter resistance as you carry out the plan, leaf your way back through these pages and set yourself back up to create a supportive environment that encourages focus and commitment for you.

Lastly, I want to stress again the power of mindset and self-reflection in maintaining balance. Your thoughts and beliefs play a significant role in your overall well being and your ability to stay focused on your goals as well as motivate you to keep going. Cultivate a growth mindset that embraces progress over perfection, practice self-reflection, regularly evaluating your efforts and celebrating your achievements.

By nurturing a positive mindset, you'll find the motivation and resilience to keep moving forward. And for me, I believe having the help of a life coach is a great way to always be nurturing a positive mindset. Having balance in life and with how you spend your time is not a destination to be reached, but finding balance in your life plan is an ongoing journey, but with the right mindset focus and self-awareness, the tools you've been given here, you can create a harmonious, fulfilling life that encompasses all the pillars of Divine Time.

CHAPTER 14

How to Maintain Your Divine Time System + Help

Here you are! You've identified time bombs and taken steps to audit your time and make difficult choices on your goals and priorities. You've crafted your motherhood mission statement and have it as a guiding light, and given focus to the 5 pillars setting into motion the ideas it sparked. You understand that taking time for yourself is a sacred action and that balance is essential in progressing in your use of Divine Time.

You've done an incredible job. Even if you've just read up to this point with the intention to come back through later and complete the activities, you will find that more awareness of your thoughts about time will begin to change how you show up in your life.

This chapter is all about the essential steps to maintaining your Divine Time System. By implementing these strategies, you'll ensure that your system, all the knowledge you've gained and lessons learned, as well as using the practical tools continues to work for you in the long run

Regular Check-ins

The first step in maintaining your Divine Time System is to have regular check-ins with yourself and your personalized plan worksheet and evaluate where it all stands for you. Life is constantly changing and our priorities evolve along the way. It's crucial to set aside time for reflection and reevaluation. I personally think once a quarter works, that's what works for me.

But I know others pick times like at the start of a new school year or as summer comes. Many moms like to check-in and evaluate at that time too.

Choose a time in the near future, perhaps three months from now and assess how your Divine Time System is working for you. Reflect on what's working well and what needs adjustment. Are there any goals that are no longer aligned with your current desires? By staying attuned to these changes, you can adapt your system to fit your evolving needs.

Recommit

The second step in maintaining the Divine Time System is to recommit to your goals. Just as we set goals at the beginning of our journey, we need to reaffirm our dedication to them regularly. There is no better, more driving feeling to get you into action and to keep going than the feeling of commitment.

Take time to revisit how you're spending your time and perhaps redo the time tracker and audit your time again and recommit to doing that for a week. Maybe there's a new time bomb that's going off for you that wasn't there before and it needs to be diffused.

Evaluate your time goals and assess their relevance and importance in your life. Are they still aligned with your values and priorities that were set when we created your mission back in the previous chapters? If so, re-commit to them with a renewed enthusiasm. And if not, don't hesitate to adjust or set new goals that better reflect your current mission.

Self-Compassion and Grace

The third and final step in maintaining your divine time system cannot be stressed enough from me: You have to possess so much self-compassion and grace for yourself when you don't always hit the mark.

Perfection is something that we will experience in heaven, and as long as we are human and living on this earth, there will be trouble. There will be challenges, and there will be this truth that we are amazing and at times we will also feel like a mess. Let's not go into our maintenance plan thinking that the goal is to 100% understand it all or reach it and then keep it at a high level forever. Remember that living Divine Time is a state of action we are in, so if you are living into its principles even 70-80% of the time, that will be amazing for your busy mom life.

How about we see it as striving for more of rolling hills where we are going after taking control of our time? Some days we'll forget to remember what we know or will allow a time bomb to keep us from our goal.

You've been given all you need to really impact your view of time and how you use it for more. I encourage you not to go on this journey of creating your divine time plan and maintaining it alone.

Help With Maintaining Your Divine Time System

I am so happy for you and proud of you for following what was outlined here for you in the pages of this book. Time truly is our most precious resource and the time we have to use here on earth is a gift from God to be used with care.

You have enhanced your relationship with time, followed the divine time saving process, overcome time bombs, and created your personalized Divine Time saving plan. You now have what you need to take back control of your time whenever you decide to, plus the three steps to call upon so you can maintain this control of your time.

And though I know you are capable of being successful with all that is offered here, I also want you to know that I am here for you if you want to have more help, support and personalize guidance and also get the results you want faster.

I personally like to work with someone as a team because I get to my goals more quickly, more easily, and it's just simply more fun to not have to go it alone. As a certified life coach who is a Catholic mom and an expert at helping moms have more control of all the aspects of a busy mom life, working together will provide you numerous benefits.

You'll have a coach to help you remove obstacles you don't see, share insights with you from years of experience, and offer guidance that can make a significant difference in your ability to stay on track. As a professional life coach, I can offer a fresh perspective, accountability, and encouragement as you go through the Divine TIme Solution. I can help you navigate challenges with maintaining control of your time, and brainstorm solutions with you.

And my favorite part is to be there to celebrate your achievements along the way!

When it comes to following through and maintaining a Divine Time System, working together can be invaluable. Even beyond time management, I have expertise and tools to share necessary for success in all the other areas of your life inside of my life coaching offerings. Take all you've learned here at Divine Time and may it greatly bless your motherhood.

And if you decide that check-ins, progress tracking, and ongoing support from a life coach who can keep you motivated even during challenging times and to fine tune your divine time system, then I invite you to reach out via danielle@daniellethienel.com or visit www.daniellethienel.com. Thank you for joining me in *The Divine Time Solution*. May God bless you and your busy mom life.

CHAPTER 15

Living Life Through the Lens of Divine Time

When you live your life through the lens of Divine TIme, life looks different. It is much more intentional, slower-paced, and spiritual because it requires your whole being. You need to engage your mind, your faith principles, and what you know and believe about God and how He can help us.

Divine Time is about increasing our communication pathways with Him. It's not rushed and I find it a more joyful way to live! It forces you to be present in each moment. This is what I teach my clients as I help them navigate the challenges and joys of life. If you'd like the same assistance, it all starts with an email to danielle@daniellethienel.com. You can also visit www.daniellethienel.com.

When I live by Divine Time, I find that I am more grateful and decisive. Instead of focusing purely on productivity and end results, I have found this way to bring more peace in the journey.

Our typical approach to time treats it as a commodity to be managed and optimized, but I see it as a sacred resource that is a gift from God to be used wisely and purposefully. I seek to treat time as I would a friend, speaking kindly and positively about my relationship with time. This perspective can affect shifts to your daily tasks and choices in a way that can bring peace and fulfillment.

Using my personal mission statement as a measure of each choice I make with my time has helped me channel the peace of Christ within my coaching practice and within my own motherhood journey.

Where the typical decision-making matrix relied heavily on personal preferences and immediate benefits, I feel divinely guided in the decisions I make, and I know the same can be true for you. When you seek divine guidance in your decisions—both big and small—by praying, reflecting, and asking for God's wisdom and direction, your decisions are aligned. It allows you to be decisive and confident in your path forward.

As I live by Divine Time, I look at rest and renewal differently than I used to. I remember waiting until everything else was done and completed before taking time for myself—if I even got to that point. Now, I know that integrating self-care and periods of rest as sacred, scheduled appointments are essential to enjoying your life.

Instead of focusing solely on productivity as what brings validation and acknowledgement of self-worth, I know that not treating yourself as a robot is the key to living in the way God intended us to experience this life on earth. He wants us to experience peace and patience alongside our productivity, not constant busyness and fatigue.

While other time management systems direct your focus to your output and efficiency in a way that often leads to burnout, Divine Time prioritizes the quality of your time over the quantity of tasks you complete. I don't mean that we can shirk all responsibilities in the name of living a balanced life—we still have responsibilities and it will always feel good to accomplish things off our to-do list. Divine Time is what allows us to be more purposeful and intentional with the moments in our day.

Perhaps that looks like putting your phone away more or being 100% present during your next family vacation. This could even look like expressing more gratitude to God for being where you are in life.

I remember before practicing Divine Time, I felt angry a lot of the time about the overwhelm and stress I was experiencing. I often felt lacking in the joys I wanted and also that time was always scarce. It was never ruthless—just this clock that was always ticking, going by too fast. Now, I hold time in such high regard because it's a precious gift that is limited. I approach time as a valued relationship in my life.

As I shared earlier in this book, I used to never pause for prayer or quiet moments. Now, morning time is my habitual one-on-one time with God. And again, I remind you of the helpful prayer that will keep you aligned with God's Divine Time:

Holy Spirit, come into my heart where you already abide. Please guide my thoughts, feelings, and actions today and may they align with God's will. Please make my crooked path straight.

May The Divine Time Solution lift you to a higher, holier way of living with peace and patience in your daily life.

About the Author

Danielle is a wife, mom, and member of the Catholic faith. She was introduced to life coaching at a very overwhelming stage of motherhood and had so much positive transformation through having a life coach's help, and the effective tools and strategies it brings, she then became a certified life coach herself. For the last 5 years she has made it her mission to now help other struggling moms more easily navigate the complexities of motherhood with grace and confidence.

She is also the author of *The Cyclone Mom Method*® and *The Peaceful Mind Bible for Busy Moms*. Additionally, she hosts a popular weekly podcast giving moms a path to find the peace, balance, and joy they crave in their everyday lives.

In *The Divine Time Solution*, Danielle delves into the heart of one of the biggest struggles moms bring to her life coaching sessions: time management. As a coach who has worked with countless women, she knows firsthand how essential it is to not continue with conventional time management options but instead manage it from the inside out, which this book addresses.

In her free time, Danielle loves to hang out with her husband at their pool, support her children in all their fun endeavors, travel the world (she's taken three trips to Europe in recent years) and she also has a deep affection for the beach, where she will always find relaxation and inspiration.

To connect with Danielle, find out more about her current life coaching offerings, or inquire about speaking engagement availability, visit her at www.daniellethienel.com or send an email to danielle@daniellethienel.com.

Acknowledgements

Ifirst acknowledge our Lord God Almighty for the blessings He has bestowed on me and my family. I continue to be in awe of His continual inspirations, love and abundance making it possible to be in the position to create books and do all the other things I love to do.

To my dad, who in the year this book was produced, passed away from this earth and has undoubtedly taken his seat in heaven. I'm forever grateful for all the Divine Time we spent together as we both made the most of every moment together creating exceptional experiences full of love and laughter.

To my first and forever best friend Jill. You too are now in heaven, however, I thank you for all of the great times we shared, both in our childhood and once motherhood arrived for us both. My sadness of your passing was a catalyst for The Divine Time Solution so my legacy of this book is your legacy too.

To my husband, my teammate in life and ever present supporter. Thank you with all my heart for always being my number one cheerleader. There isn't a day that goes by where you are not on the top of my gratitude list.

To my children, may you be inspired to live your life by Divine Time so you keep God first and also keep focus on not just important items, but instead on things that truly matter. I hope we have lots and lots of time together, but no matter the length it ends up being, my time with you has been my absolute favorite. I love you all more than words can say.

To Kim, we have done it yet again. Partnering with your gifts and talents always has me saying, "She was the perfect person to be paired with!" Thank you for being the essential piece to what I couldn't have completed as well without you.

Milton Keynes UK
Ingram Content Group UK Ltd.
UKHW031001231024
450026UK00011B/670